JOARA

A TALE OF THE NEW WORLD

JOHN HARRIS BRADLEY

ISBN 979-8-9895522-2-1 Paperback
ISBN 979-8-9895522-3-8 Ebook

Published 2024

CONTENTS

JOARA

ARCHEOLOGICAL, ANTHROPOLOGIC AND HISTORICAL PERSPECTIVE

*Joara*_is a fictional account of the first Spanish attempt to colonize the interior of southeastern North America. Although fiction, the account is tightly woven around recent factual discoveries relating to Captain Juan Pardo's Expedition of 1566-67.

For years, controversy had stirred over the route taken through the southeast of North America by Hernando de Soto in 1540, with his hundreds of Spanish conquistadors and a few thousand native mercenaries.

In the mid-1980's, the late renowned archeologist and historian, Charles Hudson, and his colleagues at the University of Georgia began to successfully argue that de Soto's route into the Appalachians followed the Catawba River Valley through South and North Carolina rather than the previously favored Savannah River Valley between Georgia and South Carolina. It was also recognized that Captain Juan Pardo's Expedition of 1566-67, followed de Soto's route and established a number of forts along the way. All this was confirmed by careful study and translation by Paul Hoffman, of original documents of Capt. Pardo's official notary, Juan de la Bandera, as found in the Spanish archives in Sevilla and in the North Carolina Office of Archives and History in Raleigh.

In 1986, a young archeologist inspired by Charles Hudson, Davide Moore, did extensive excavations at two sites in the Catawba River Valley. Although his excavations did not confirm an early Spanish presence, Moore did demonstrate that both sites were large villages with earthen ceremonial mounds.

In 1994, David Moore and another young archeologist, Robin Beck, discovered 16th-century Spanish ceramics and iron nails at one of the sites that Moore had earlier explored in 1986. This site was identified as the "Berry Site" after the cooperating family who owned the property. The

Berry Site is located eight miles north of Morganton, NC. Subsequent excavations at the Berry Site have revealed more Spanish ceramics, lead balls, chain armor, and a set of cast iron scales.

In 1997, an underground gradiometer survey was conducted revealing evidence of four large burned buildings. This has since been confirmed by yearly excavations since 2003 by the Exploring Joara Foundation.

Now, in 2023, it is a foregone conclusion that the Berry Site is the location of the Chiefdom of Joara, visited by both Hernando de Soto and Juan Pardo. The last small remnant of the grand ceremonial mound was plowed under by a farmer in the last century, but we know where it was, and a stone's throw away lie the buried burned-out remains of Fort San Juan.

The three Berry Site archeologists, Davide Moore, Robin Beck and Christopher Roding wrote, in an Afterword to Charles Hudson's, *The Juan Pardo Expeditions*, "If Berry does indeed contain the remains of Fort San Juan, then its burned buildings offer a window onto a single historical event: the fiery destruction of the fort and the end of Spanish colonial ambitions in northern La Florida."

INTRODUCTION
&
NARRATIVE PERSPECTIVE OF
ENDOVÉLICO

Although the book *Joara* can stand alone as an accurate, but fictionalized, portrayal of the Spanish aborted attempt to colonized the piedmont and mountains of the southeast, the stories of its four main protagonists, three young Jewish men and an older Spanish Gypsy, are told in the prequel to *Joara* entitled *Belmonte*. A very short synopsis is as follows:

> Destiny weaves tight the fates of three young Portuguese men and an older Spanish Gypsy. All must flee Iberia, but first all must participate in one last act; the rendering of Justice to a murderer.

The particular old-world paradigm as portrayed in the first book, *Belmonte*, was a peculiar Judeo/Templar world view at play in first four centuries of the *intentional* nation of Portugal, begun in 1128. I say "*intentional*" because Portugal was created, from concept to physical reality, by the Templar victors of the first Crusade to re-capture Jerusalem from the Muslims. (1096-1099 AD) The spiritual experiment of Portugal, beginning in 1128, was sponsored and endowed by Saint Bernard and the French Templar leaders.

Templar virtues and values and an alternate interpretation of Christian history, were promoted for 382 years by an unbroken sequence of Portuguese Kings, beginning in 1128 and ending in 1521. Many of these Portuguese Kings were Masters of the Temple.

Templar virtues and values found expression through sailing into unknown waters in ventures of discovery and commerce. An international banking system was created. Wherever the Portuguese went, they intermarried. Trade was more important than conquest. Spiritually, the Templars focused on the Holy Spirit, as manifest by Christ, but common to all religions.

The Templar mind-set would embrace the virtues of truth, beauty, dignity and honor, with little respect for stale habit, dogmatism, and bigotry. The Kings and Princes of Portugal , associated with the Templar Order, the Order of Aviz and the Order of Christ, were the vanguard of the Portuguese age of discovery and prosperity. This set the standard for the adventuresome people of Portugal who followed their lead in vast numbers.

Pre-dating this Templar overlay upon the land of Lusitania, and pre-dating the Islamic culture of southern Portugal, was a pre-Roman/Judaic culture. The origin of this ancient Judaic culture of Portugal is a mystery yet to be solved. One of the epicenters of this old Hebrew influence was the hilltop town of Belmonte, located behind Serra da Estrela range in central Portugal near the border with Spain.

Within the span of ten years, three defining events occurred in Portugal:

> In 1496, King Manuel I ordered all the Jews in Portugal who refused to be baptized to be expelled.

> In 1500, Brazil was discovered by Pedro Álvares Cabral of Belmonte, and Portugal commenced to create its Maritime Empire with direct commercial trading with the orient and Brazil.

> In 1506, over 2000 Jews were massacred in Lisbon over Easter weekend.

Fifty years later Portugal's "glory days" were fading and the once-fresh Vision of Portugal's Templar founders had dimmed from common memory replaced with vainglory, corruption and fanaticism. This is the ambient of the book, *Belmonte*.

To relate the stories of *Belmonte* I felt that I needed the voice of story-telling narrator, a voice out of the Lusitanian past, maneuvering through history yet transcending it. An image came to mind from the Anthropological Museum in the Jerónimous Monastery in the Belém neighborhood of Lisbon. It was a Roman era bust of the Iron Age shaman called Endovélico.. He was a legendary god-like healer, a mover in both the Overworld and the Underworld. One of Endovélico's specialties was what is called *incubation*, an ancient practice whereby the believer seeking help would sleep in, or near, the temple of a god or goddess, with the expectation that the deity would visit the supplicant in dreamtime, giving guidance and inspiration. The cult of Endovélico was so popular among the ancient Lusitanians that, when the Romans occupied the land, rather than suppress the cult, they promoted it and participated in it.

I used the character of Endovélico as a *deus ex machina*. I gave him a personality, part angelic and part human, living in an Imaginal Realm, and defying space and time on a whim. He became a Lord of Dreams, a supernatural historian and storyteller.

The two protagonists from Belmonte, Ruy and Davide, age 17, were, before leaving for their first year at the university in Coimbra, enjoying their last boyhood summer as shepherds on the side of a mountain, tending the sheep of Davide's father. They discover a massive sculpted boulder and make it their camp site, sleeping on the smooth flat top of the rock in two sepulcher-like shallow tubs carved in the stone. They learn that the place is called the "Rock of Endovélico, "and soon afterward, they are visited by the Lord of Dreams.

Endovélico challenges each boy with a gift. The gift is that each choose from history an event that he is most curious about, and, after falling asleep, Endovélico will appear and take him back in time to witness that curious event. Endovélico sets the stage and lets the boys witness history firsthand.

I found in this character, Endovélico, the perfect story telling voice I was looking for, always lurking, eavesdropping and taking botes nehind the scenes of history.

I liked Endovélico so much that, in *Joara,* on occasion, he enters as a narrating voice, not as a Lusitanian, but as a shaman, or a Frenchman who has managed to survive by integrating into a local tribe. In one respect the transition from an old European mind-set and a Native-American world-view was natural, because both share a due respect for the supernatural.

The book *Joara* resumes the story of *Belmonte* after the four protagonists, Ruy, Davide, Daniel and the Gypsy Juancinto avenge the murder of Daniel's parents. The murderer, Captain Raul Estigarriba, employed by the Inquisition, is left to die, deep in the vast labyrinthian swampland known as the "Doñana", located just east of the harbor of Sanlucar de Barremeda, Spain.

Miles from any human ear, Estigarriba is left howling for mercy, naked and bound to the earth with his body covered in honey, attracting flies, rats, mongoose and lynx.

The foursome return to Sanlucar and make contact with Captain Juan Pardo, who accepts them as soldiers/colonists for the major Armada of 17 ships to La Florida, scheduled to leave in a week's time, o April 19, 1566

Lined up with 19 other vessels outside of the harbors of Cadiz and Sanlucar, their frigate, *El Redimido* raised its sails and lurched forward toward the west. The four members of the newly founded brotherhood consider themselves as survivors.

On arriving in La Florida they meet a true survivor; a young Frenchman called Guillermo Rufín, an actual historical character, who had survived in five years in La Florida by marrying into an Indian tribe.

Daniel tries to initiate a conversation with Rufín:

"My friends and I are exiles from the Iberian Peninsula. We are here to seek a new life in the New World. Our only escape was with the big Armada that left from Sanlucar."

"Really?", the Frenchman replied with some contempt. "You do not know what's in store for you here?"

"Maybe not, " answered Daniel. "But we are survivors," he countered.

"The only survivors I know around here are Indian, " the Frenchman assured him with a smirk. "Are you prepared to become an Indian?"

CHAPTER 1

THE PASSAGE ACROSS THE SOUTH ATLANTIC

APRIL TO JULY 1566

Ruy hoped the Armada's "*rota*" to the New World would take them due west from Spain to the Açores and then to La Florida. If so, perhaps he could glimpse Prince Henry's School for Navigators as they sailed by the cliffs of Sagres, the western-most point of Portugal and continental Europe. He could say a proper good-bye to his "*saudages*"[1] and dreams of becoming a Portuguese navigator, say farewell to his love and family and homeland. But no, he should have known the Spanish armada took a course due south, and by sunset he could see the gleaming gold-orange cliffs of the coast of Morocco.

The fleet followed the African shore for over a week and then cruised over to the Grand Canaries and the island of Santa Cruz and then to the port of Tenerife. At the port, they spent a few days resupplying meat, water, and making last-minute repairs. From the Canaries, La Florida lay due west across the vast Ocean Sea. Ruy thought to himself, '*a hundred years ago, such a voyage would be unimaginable, and even if you could have had it planned and financed it, you could not have found seamen brave enough to risk sailing off the edge of the flat world. But now, good winds and decent weather, the New World was only a month away.*' Ruy knew this, but even now, he noticed the soldiers and the crew were anxious and uneasy, and those who had prayer beads spent much time fiddling with them.

The crew aboard the *Redimido* numbered about ten, and there were 30 soldiers as part of Juan Pardo's command of 250. The Captain of the *Redimido*, Nuno de Faria, being Portuguese, got along very well with Daniel, who, to the Captain, seemed to know everything about the frigate as if he had built it and sailed it before. Daniel even prevailed upon Captain Faria to let Ruy help him with the daily navigation charts. Keeping these charts was perhaps unnecessary or redundant because every day at sunset all the Captains of the ships in the Armada met with Captain-General Archiniegra on the mother ship.

Archiniegra's Master Pilot was in charge, and all the other ships had no orders but to follow. After sailing for three days down the African coast, Captain Juan Pardo left his galleon, the *San Salvador*, to spend a day and night aboard the caravel, *Redimido*, to become more familiar with his soldiers.

Some of the crew and soldiers noticed the fact that Juan Pardo, when speaking with Captain Faria, Ruy, David, Daniel, and a few others, talked to them in fluent Portuguese. This was perceived as an offense; thus, seeds of jealously and division began to spread among the Spanish crew and passengers. When cornered by soldiers, Ruy, David, and Daniel freely confessed that they were Portuguese. The soldiers did not question their religion, probably because they did not care. National pride was a far weightier factor than religion. Ruy, David, and Daniel managed to pacify their suspicions that they were spies. Daniel was particularly good at portraying to the crew and soldiers that they, like most of humanity, were victims of Established Injustice.

Their fellow soldiers, now "*compañeros*," soon began to express their contempt for rival Portugal with salacious jests and insinuations about the 12-year-old King of Portugal named Sebastian. The rumor had spread throughout Spain, perhaps stemming from the Spanish royal palace in Valladolid, that the present and future King of Portugal, this 12-year-old boy, orphaned by his father, abandoned by his mother, and under the oversight of his grandmother, was being raised at court by two brothers, both being Jesuit priests and known homosexuals. Sebastian was being raised to hate women and to keep close company with the priests of God.

When confronted with this gossip, Ruy, David, and Daniel claimed, quite correctly, that they were barely familiar with these rumors about little King Sebastian, but that it would not surprise them if the stories were true, and that, indeed, it did not forebode well for the future of Portugal. They let it be known that this shame about Portugal was one of the many reasons that they had decided to cast their futures with the "manly" aspirations of the nobility of Spain. A few of the soldiers were still suspicious.

To prove and certify that the rumored disease of the young king of Portugal was not contagious among the nationals of that homeland, some of the crew demanded that the three young Portuguese expatriates relate to their fellow soldiers something of their own personal sexual escapades. This was particularly easy for Daniel, who took the lead. He talked at length, to the fascination of his new comrades, about the differences involved in seducing Portuguese women versus Spanish women versus Moorish women versus Berber women, versus, etc. The recount of Daniel's escapades was a difficult act for Ruy to follow. He resolved to tell the truth rather than lie. He said that he had had only one love in his life, described all her virtues, and how, of necessity, he had had to leave the *love of his life* six months ago to join his new comrades in this great adventure.

Davide had more trouble, and like Ruy, opted for the unvarnished truth: he was a virgin. His crewmates sympathized with his plight; then and there, they resolved to remedy the sad situation as soon as possible.

On the first night in Tenerife, Davide's new-found friends took him to a notorious whorehouse. For a few seconds, upon realizing where his comrades were taking him, Davide thought about protesting. Then he realized that, after being a participant in a murder, he had thrown in his lot with those who believed in a just and merciful God. If this gracious Lord would have mercy on his capital crime in the pursuit of justice then surely the same deity would have some charity left over to overlook and accommodate an act of sex without love in order to consolidate the unity of his new brotherhood. Davide left his virginity behind in Tenerife.

The voyage across the Ocean Sea was peaceful until they encountered a major storm 15 days out from the Canaries and a week from the port in San Juan. There were a few moments when the three boys thought they would be sacrificed at sea. Davide's prayers were followed by those of Ruy and Daniel, although said with less intensity and precision.

The *Redimido* fared well with no damage, but Captain Pardo's ship, the *San Salvador*, lost a mast, and the *Redimido* followed the *San Salvador*, as she limped into the harbor at San Juan, Puerto Rico. The three exiles stepped down the gangplank onto the dock, led by the Gypsy, Juancinto Taranto, who, at his own request, now called himself in public "Juan Martín de Badajoz." Juancinto was tired of standing out as a Gypsy in an anti-Gypsy world. He resolved that in the "New World" he would not be mistreated due to his name.

At the busy port of San Juan, white Spanish overlords directed black African and brown Taino Indian slaves in a hubbub of activity surrounded by a cacophony of sounds and colors with floating waves of fragrance from pungent tobacco and ginger to soft cocoa and cotton. Among the slaves, there was an order of ascendency with the blacks, sinewy and robust with hot iron brands stamped on their foreheads, speaking Spanish fluently and interacting with their masters while, at the bottom of the social ladder, Native Indian slaves executing orders in silence.

Within a week repairs were made to the *San Salvador* and Captain Archiniegra, having received orders from Captain-General Menéndez in Havana, dispatched Juan Pardo, with his three ships and 250 men to stop at the new colony at San Augustín and then proceed up the coast of Florida to reinforce the new fort at Santa Elena.

CHAPTER 2

SANTA ELENA

JULY - NOVEMBER 1566

Guillermo Rufín, a young Frenchman, found himself aboard the *Redimido* for the three-day trip up the coast from San Augustín to to the new fort at Santa Elena. Rufín had been assigned by Adelantado Menéndez to help Captain Juan Pardo as an interpreter for the Indians. In addition, Rufín was aboard the *Redimido* to perform the duties of a pilot, because, a few years previous, he had helped pilot a French frigate to Santa Elena, to the now demolished French fort. He guided the three ships along the channel as they meandered through the marsh grass, leading the way to *terra firma* and the new Spanish fort, which had replaced the French fort.

Daniel observed this Frenchman from the minute he boarded the *Redimido*. He noticed that the young man, probably not older than himself, comported himself with absolute confidence and ease that was at odds with the apprehension emanating from the rest of the crew. After listening to the crew's scuttlebutt, Daniel learned that the young man had been a survivor of the earlier French fort on the island and could speak the language of the local Indians.

At the first opportunity, Daniel approached Rufín and said, "Hello, my name is Daniel. I hear you are French. Do you speak Spanish?"

"About as well as you do," was the reply.

"Well, yes, I am Portuguese. I guess you can hear my accent. But you are French, am I right? I thought the Spanish were at war with France, at least here in La Florida."

"That may be true, but I am at war with no-one. But you, you are Portuguese. I thought the Spanish and Portuguese were like Cain and Abel, mortal enemies around the world. What are you doing here, working for your enemy?"

"My friends and I are exiles from the Iberian Peninsula. We are here to seek a new life in the New World. Our only escape was with the big armada that left from Sanlucar."

"Really?" the Frenchman replied with some contempt. "You do not know what's in store for you here?"

"Maybe not," answered Daniel. "But we are survivors," he countered.

"The only survivors I know around here are Indian," the Frenchman assured him with a smirk. "Are you prepared to become an Indian?"

Daniel could not answer this, so he tried to change the subject. "I understand you speak the language of the Indians?"

"I speak a dialect from the nearby village of Orista. Every village has its own dialect. I can understand most of them here on the coast, but when you go into the interior, following the rivers up into the hill country, the language changes. I was learning the hill country languages up until two years ago when the Spanish Captain de Roja came with his men and found me and took me to Havana, and then it was all Spanish. I'll be relieved to get back home again."

"You mean to Santa Elena?

The Frenchman turned and looked at Daniel straight in the eye, and whispered with the power of a shout, "Hell no! My home is up the river in Orista. I have a wife and son there, and my father-in-law is the chief of the village."

Daniel was taken aback trying to assimilate this revelation, when the Frenchman, smiled and said, "I have to go. I hear Captain Pardo calling my name."

"But wait. Tell me, what is your name," Daniel countered.

"Which one?" the Frenchman grinned.

"The one you were born with," Daniel replied.

"I was christened with the name, Guillaume Rouffi, but the Spanish call me Guillermo Rufín, or Rufín for short. Now in the village they call me something else," Rufín smiled and disappeared.

In the late afternoon sun, Daniel watched Rufín guide the helmsman from the ocean into a vast natural harbor and straight toward a prominence of land, like an island between two rivers. The *Redimido* led the way for the larger galleons through the marsh grass channel to the muddy dock, which was the port of Santa Elena. Unlike the barren rocky beach of San Augustín, Santa Elena was a flat green island of tall pines and enormous mossy live oak trees, a land of promise protruding out of a sea of alligator-infested marsh grass.

It was only two months previous, in May, that Adelantado Menéndez had visited Santa Elena, during which he commanded the building of a large wooden fort with a stockade and six cannons. While nearing completion Menéndez had left his kinsman, Esteban de Las Alas, in charge of the new fort, which was christened, "Fort San Felipe".

Always on the move, Adelantado Menéndez set out from Santa Elena for San Augustín along the inland waterway with his indispensable interpreter, Guillermo Rufín, and a small party of soldiers with Indian guides. They arrived at San Augustín and waited two months to the arrival of Captain-General Archiniegra's great Armada in July. When the Armada did arrive, Menéndez wasted no time. He immediately directed Captain Juan Pardo, with three ships, to sail up the coast to Santa Elena. Guillermo Rufín was assigned as an interpreter for the Santa Elena expedition. When Pardo's three ships arrived in Santa Elena, they were met with a sad and appalling sight. The "well supplied" garrison of 110 men that Adelantado Menédez had left at the new Fort San Felipe just two months previous had disappeared. Captain de Las Alas welcomed Captain Juan Pardo, stepping off the gangplank as somewhat of a Savior. And indeed he was, for shortly after Menéndez had left Santa Elena, in May, a supply ship from San Augustín arrived. When it did, 60 of the 110 men mutinied and commandeered the ship and all the supplies, then set sail for Cuba.

20 more men deserted the colony and fled into the interior, leaving Las Alas with only 30 hungry men to hold the fort against an expected assault from French Corsairs. The storehouse was bare, and the crop harvest had been disappointing. Now the soldiers were left depending on food from the meager supply the friendly Indians left for them. However, the Indians were losing patience. When Pardo's three ships arrived, the men of Fort San Felipe were on the verge of starvation, and they welcomed the expedition as their salvation.

Pardo and Las Alas worked well together, and between them they corrected the food shortage, restored order, and reinforced the fort. Ruy, Daniel, and Daniel were not accustomed to hard work in the mid-summer heat and humidity of Santa Elena. Digging moats and erecting a stockade sapped their strength. Guillermo Rufín worked by their side but seemed to be far more comfortable, often taking a break to converse with visiting Indians, and complaining under his breath that he needed leave to go to his village to see his wife and son.

After listening to Rufín's growing gripe for a week, Captain Pardon finally permitted him to visit Orista, his Indian town, 15 miles up the river. Witnessing this, Ruy and Daniel then privately cornered the captain and argued that they should be assigned to accompany Rufín because of his importance to the mission as an interpreter, to make sure he would return to the fort. They argued their case well and won.

The next morning Rufín procured a canoe and the three set off for a three-day trip to Orista and back. Paddling against the slow current, they arrived at the village in four hours. Rufín was exuberant because their visit happened to coincide with a festival called "*Toya*."

He explained to his new two new friends, "There will be a feast tonight with drama, dancing, and cavorting, followed in the morning by the ceremony of the '*Toya*' in which three men of the village will go into the wilds for a few days in quest for visions and remedies for the problems facing the village."

Ruy and Daniel took advantage of the privacy of the canoe trip to begin quizzing Rufín about his curious past. Rufín explained that he had been orphaned as a child. A friend of his parents, the French Captain Jean Ribault, took Rufín under his wing when he was 15. That was four years ago. Captain Ribault permitted him to sign on as cabin boy on what was the first expedition to Santa Elena. He explained that they had come from Normandy with two ships and 160 men. They constructed a fort called Charlesfort near the one the Spanish were currently building.

Rufín explained: "It was soon evident that we could not grow, buy, or steal provisions enough for 160 men, so after only one month Captain Ribault decided to sail back to France to bring back more supplies. The captain asked for volunteers to stay, and only 28 of us agreed to stay while 132 men went back to France with the Captain. I stayed. Why would I want to go back to France? They killed my parents."

"They killed your parents? Why?" asked Ruy.

"Well, I'd rather not say because most Spanish would not comprehend."

Daniel interjected, "Guillermo. Don't you remember when we talked earlier? We are not Spanish. There is a difference. We are Portuguese."

"Yes, but you're still Catholic, right?"

Ruy and Daniel laughed so hard that they almost capsized the canoe.

"What's so funny?" Rufín demanded.

"Guillermo. We are Jews!", Daniel managed to say between guffaws. "Ruy, me, and Davide are all Portuguese Jews running from the Catholic Inquisition, and Juan Martín, he's a Gypsy who's running with us. I would have thought you would have figured that out by now!"

"No, I guess not. In France, we did not have much of an Inquisition against Jews. I don't know any Jews. But the Catholics are killing my people, including my parents."

"Who are your people, Guillermo? I'm confused", Ruy asked.

Rufín replied, "Jean Ribault, and most of us who came with him from France to live in this New World . . . well, we are Huguenots."

"Huguenots?" exclaimed Ruy, "What's a 'huge nut?' I have never heard of a Huguenot. What are they?"

"Huguenots don't believe in the Catholic form of Christianity, with Rome and the Pope and the Holy Roman Empire with the King of Spain as the head of it. They call us Protestants. We trace our beliefs back to the Cathars in Provence and before that to the first disciples of Christ, but that's all I can tell you because I'm not really a Huguenot anymore."

"What are you then?" Ruy asked.

"I'm not anything. Why do I have to be something?"

"Let me put it another way, 'What are you comfortable with?'"

"I'm comfortable with not going back to France. I'm comfortable living in my village with nature, spirits, kindred spirits, and one over-all Great Spirit. That's what I am comfortable with. That's how I like it. You'll see."

"So, what happened to the 28 volunteers who stayed here waiting for Jean Ribault to return?" Daniel changed the subject.

"Well, Jean Ribault said he would return in six months, and that's about how much food we had in the storehouse for 28 people. In January of 1563, the food ran out. That's when I decided to go live with the Indians in Orista. I had spent my time learning their language, and I was sent to Orista and the other villages to negotiate, or really beg, for food.

The Indians were generous, but the food they gave burned up in a fire in a storehouse we had built.

"The Indians took that as a bad sign for the French colony, and maybe a good sign for them to be rid of the foreigners. They had a vision of trouble, and indeed, there was. The men were hopeless and desperate, and the man who Captain Ribault had left in charge, Captain Albert de la Pierria, could not handle the situation. He demanded strict law and order and started hanging men for minor offenses. The soldiers mutinied and chased Pierria through the woods. They caught him and killed him.

"The chiefs and medicine men from Orista and Escamacu, and even the leaders of the Guale people to the south, pitied the soldiers of Charlesfort and came up here to help and advise them. The chiefs announced that their best future was to go back to France, so, with the wood from the fort, the Indians helped the soldiers build a makeshift sloop. The Escamacu supplied the soldiers with rope for the rigging. They used hanging-moss and coal tar pitch for the caulking. And from Guale, where they weave nice mats and blankets, they made sails out of light natural fibers. They supplied the boat with corn and beans and fishing tools. Can you believe it? When I was in Havana, I heard that sloop had made it all the way to Europe!

"They were picked up by an English ship and taken back to England for interrogation. So, they survived, but not all of them. In the middle of the Atlantic, with the doldrums, the soldiers drew lots to see which of them would be cannibalized for the survival of the rest. And wouldn't you know it, it was one of my friends who we had saved from being hanged by the judgement of Captain Pierria . . . well, his flesh was divided up among the other 26 soldiers."

"So, why did you not go with them? "asked Daniel.

"As I told you, I was not going back to France. What did I have there? Here I had a whole village that has adopted me. But I didn't tell that to the men of Charlesfort. They were too foolish and desperate to comprehend. I told them that I was not going with them because not one of them, of all 27, had any navigation experience. That they would be totally at the mercy of the winds and currents, and that they would never get back to Europe alive. But they did, the old medicine man from my village had seen it in a vision. I knew this, but I didn't tell them because I did not want to go back to the country that had killed my parents."

"So, you went back to Orista?" Ruy asked.

"Of course! I went to my village and I married a beautiful girl, the oldest daughter of the Cacique. After a time, we had a son. I was never happier. It was the best year of my life. Then two years ago, the Spanish came to Santa Elena looking for the old French fort. It was an expedition led by Captain Hernando de Rojas. Someone told him of my existence and where I was living. He came to Orista and kidnapped me. I showed de Rojas where Charlesfort was, and they burned what was left of it. I showed them a column that Ribault had erected a few miles from the fort, claiming the land for France. They knocked it down and took it back to Spain as proof of the French intentions. I had to tell the Spanish all about the French: their ships, their forces, their artillery, and their plans. De Rojas took me back to Havana. I stayed in Cuba until the beginning of this year when Adelantado Menéndez arrived with his Armada in Havana and insisted that I join his expedition as his chief interpreter."

"Why are you not with Menéndez now?" Daniel inquired.

"Because he thinks that Santa Elena will be his capital of all of La Florida and this part of the New World. So, he assigned me to go with Juan Pardo, because Menéndez thinks I will be more valuable working with Pardo to accomplish his ends."

"And what are those ends?" Daniel asked.

"I don't know yet, but I hear that Menéndez is due to come back to Santa Elena any day now. When he does I'm sure he will tell us."

Rufín paused for a few moments, and looking up at the backs of the two Portuguese paddling in front of him said, "Now it's my turn to ask some questions. What happened that you are running from the Inquisition in Portugal?"

Daniel, who was sitting in the middle of the canoe, began, "I am from the city of Ceuta. In case you have never heard of it, for a hundred years now Ceuta has been a Portuguese city, an enclave port city on the coast of Morocco. My mother was Jewish, and my father Muslim. Our family business, on my mother's side, was commodity trading along with the port cities of the Mediterranean South Coast. The company goes back generations, all Jewish. My Grandfather in Ceuta ran the business and the warehouse. My father ran the sea-faring operations, a handful of trading ships. He and my mother spent much of their time at sea, he as the Captain and she as the cook, not because they had to, but because they loved that life. My father taught me the art of sailing.

"Life was good, and the business thrived until last year when it attracted the vultures of the Inquisition. The Church paid pirates to seize my parent's ship at sea and throw everyone overboard."

Even Rufín winced at this thought.

Daniel thought about revealing to Rufín that he had piloted into Santa Elena the very boat the pirates had seized, but his better judgment quickly warned against the idea. He had told Rufín as much of the story as he needed to know.

Daniel continued, "So, in Ceuta, the Dominicans came after my grandfather and forced him to give them everything but his life. He is now confined to his house, and if he comes out, he has to wear a yellow dunce cap, by law. So, you see, there was no future for me in Iberia. My grandfather convinced me to go to Sanlucar and cast my fate in the New World."

"Are you married with children?" Rufín asked.

"No, I am not married."

"And you, Ruy, what's your story?"

"Davide and I are from the same area of Portugal, where at one time a lot of Jews used to live. Davide's father was a rabbi and a shepherd. My father was a doctor in a town nearby. Because practicing the Jewish faith in Portugal was against the law, you might say we were secret Jews. My father and Davide's father had business dealings with a trading company in the East Indies run by Jewish families. When the Inquisition in Goa got hold of the trading firm, they tortured the principals until they revealed every name of every Jew who had ever invested in the company. When that news got back to Lisbon, it was only a matter of time before the vultures began circling over Covilhã, where my family lived.

"As soon as my dad learned that the Inquisition was after him, he rode to Belmonte and informed Davide's father, Rabbi Elias, of the situation, telling him to go to Coimbra, where Davide and I were students at the university. He informed us that our lives were in danger. When Rabbi Elias met us in a garden in Coimbra, he had two horses ready for us with provisions and maps and everything we needed to get ourselves to Sanlucar. But he didn't even give us time to say good-bye to our friends and loved ones. I left my 'one and only' in that garden that day, and I don't expect I'll never see her again. I was going to ask her to marry me."

"And your parents, what happened to them?" Rufín inquired.

Ruy replied, "My mother died many years ago. Concerning my father, I have no news. Davide and I disappeared from Portugal almost a year ago. I have no way of knowing, but I fear the worst."

"What about the rabbi? What do you think happened to him?"

"Well, the rabbi, like my father, was a widower, and I do not think he intended to go back across the mountain to Belmonte. So, he may have figured out how to survive in Coimbra with another identity."

"Did you leave any children, Ruy?"

"Not that I know of, Guillermo."

"And Davide?"

"Well, Davide was never in love. I can tell you that, and, as the son of a rabbi, was rather pious compared to me, but I can promise that he is not a virgin so I can't guarantee that he has no offspring on the way." Roy and Daniel began laughing at this inside joke, and Daniel felt obligated to expound on how Davide lost his virginity in a whorehouse in Tenerife.

Rufín got a good laugh out of this, and by the time they had exhausted the light-hearted joking about these subjects, they were sliding into the muddy river-beach of the village of Orista, being welcomed by a joyous crowd. A villager from the bank of the river had earlier seen the canoe pass by and raced ahead along the path to informed the villagers of the imminent homecoming of their kidnapped adopted son.

Guillermo introduced his two comrades to his father-in-law, Maccon, who was known as *"Mico"* or chief. Rufín then picked up his little son, Ayamar, kissed him and said some words before turning to embrace his wife, Junica, kissing her deeply.

The village was strung out along the riverbank in circular mud-wattle houses with tree-bark roofs. At the center of the village was a large grassy clearing with two larger round structures; one was the communal house, and the other was the residence of the Mico. Since it was mid-summer, the men were barely dressed with a covering over their private parts and long hair tied up in a ball on the top of their heads. The women wore more coverings of deer-skin leather with their hair long and flowing.

In the early evening, they all feasted on fish, turkey, deer, beans, stewed peaches, and corn mush. Ruy and Daniel each had a covey of girls and young women around them, offering different nuts, fruits, and hominy cornbread, and striving for attention amidst a cacophony of giggling.

Three hours after sundown the festivities began. All the village funneled into the large communal dome and sat on benches around the perimeter, with a fire in the center and drummers to one side. Before long, there appeared men with gourd masks depicting animal spirits, dressed with fur and feathers and bells and noisemakers around their knees and ankles. They carried various wooden weapons and danced around, threatening and attacking each other and multiple members of the congregation. Some danced to the drums and made loud noises and jesters, while others walked silently and nimbly around, engaging the audience with secret meaning. The drum beating, flute playing, and dancing reached a crescendo and brought itself to a close.

This seemed to be a signal for all the young men, so disposed, to hunt down and catch hold of the girls they liked the best. Of course, this created much commotion, and frankly, Ruy and Daniel did not know how to respond. Guillermo, sensing this, suggested that each take one of Junica's sisters and spend the night with her. Daniel was glad to comply with this custom, as for the past year he had suppressed and sublimated sexual desire into a quest for revenge. Now he was ready to feel his humanity again.

Ruy, however, had been thinking of Ana Sophia ever since he referred to her on the canoe trip. The more he scanned the pretty, eager faces, the worse his *saudade* grew. Ruy finally explained his reticence to Guillermo, who then talked to a sister-in-law and her friends. Whatever Guillermo told them seemed to have the effect of eliciting their sympathy. They took Ruy by the hand and began to pull him toward the doorway. Ruy looked at Rufín, questioning what was going on. Rufín said, "They just want to help you to sleep so you can dream about your beloved."

Ruy was led into a small roundhouse and onto a large sleeping platform covered with a bearskin over a large quantity of dried oakmoss. He laid down, and the women massaged his skin with a pungent oil and gave him some sweet liquid to drink. They sang softly all around him, and the delicate, feminine fingers restored his vitality. He awoke in the morning surrounded by smiling Orista maidens, still thinking of Ana Sophia, but without a shred of guilt.

Daniel, not held back by conscience or confliction, quickly gravitated to Junica's younger sister, Sarati. This graceful, long-legged beauty beguiled him with her engaging smile and amorous eyes. She found his hand and entwined her fingers with his. She led him to the central fire and grabbed a torch, and then led him out the door toward the riverbank. With her eyes alone she beckoned him to put a canoe into the water. He followed her desire. They got in the canoe. She handed him her torch and grabbed a paddle. In a little more than a minute, she guided the craft to a small island in the river and eased it up onto the bank. Daniel pulled the canoe up onto dry ground under the branches of a flowering mimosa tree. Sarati, carrying the torch picked up some nearby rocks and used them to wedge and secure the torch in the ground.

Freed from the fire, she stood in front of Daniel and pointing to her heart; she said, "Sarati." Daniel recited the syllables of her name several times, and then pointing to his heart, said, "Daniel." She pronounced his name in a slow, laughing way and then stood in front of him and found his hands with her fine fingers. She closed her eyes and began swaying to the beat of the nearby village drum, then chanted, what seemed to Daniel, to be a prayer with his name in it. He put his hands, overlapped with hers, upon her bare hips, which swayed, more pronounced to the beat. She opened her dark eyes to see his. They came together. Sarati had never kissed a bearded man before, nor, except for her brother-in-law, been in the presence of a stranger from across the great water. She was intrigued and wanted to give herself to the experience, and besides, she was attracted to this man. They made love in the canoe until exhaustion gave way to gentle sleep. They woke at dawn and washed together in the river.

The next morning, after eating, the ceremony of Toya began. Maccon, the chief, presided over the village which gathered in the common house. After some serious talk, the drums began. Then three men appeared, dancing through the opening and around through the crowd, looking into the eyes of everyone. Guillermo explained that the men were priests, in the sense that their lives were dedicated to the spiritual welfare of the village, but they were also doctors in that they were healers, but not just of the body but also the spirit and the souls. To achieve this, they had to become intermediaries with the higher worlds. The higher worlds of Orista were ruled by god-spirit Toya.

Of the three spirit runners, one man was old, another was middle-aged, and the third was young. Rufín informed his Portuguese companions that the youngest runner was his brother-in-law, Pamayato, and he was in training to be a medicine man. As they danced to the drumbeat, the three spirit runners methodically removed their clothes. They left the common house and ran naked through the village, shouting at every dwelling, and then they took off into the dense forest, one up-river, one downriver, and one into the interior.

Rufín explained that they would run through the wilds for two days without eating. During their quest they expected to encounter visions from nature spirits, ancestors, angels, or forces from the higher worlds. After two full days of fasting and running they would return to Orista. Then the three would have a ceremony in the common house where they would, by way of magical formula, invoke Toya and make Him come and speak to them.

In this way the three spirit runners would bring fresh insight into the circumstances, welfare, and future of the village and the extended tribe. They would heal the sick, explain the past and the present, and bring prophecy for the tribe's future and some of its individuals.

Rufín explained that after the third day of the ceremony of Toya, the spirit runners would break their fast and the whole village would bring them turkey, venison, fish, corn, beans, squash and fruits, and berries from the orchards and forest. He reminded his two Portuguese friends that they could not stay for the return of the spirit runners because they had promised the captain that they would be gone only one day. However, he was staying longer, but assured them that he would relay to them any messages from the spirit runners that related to them personally or the Spanish in general. "Tell Captain Pardo that I will be back in a few days. My brother-in-law will take me to Santa Elena in his canoe."

Rufín cautioned his two new friends not to mention anything to their comrades about the pleasures they had experienced the night before. "The others would be jealous and expect the same and they would not get it only causeing trouble. So, keep your mouth closed. Make-up something boring and distasteful, and do not fail to mention that all the women are ugly."

At the garrison in Santa Elena the newly arrived soldiers from Spain passed the next two sultry summer months digging moats and building ramparts, wooden barracks and palisades. Toward the end of August, Adelantado Menéndez, the virtual King of La Florida, arrived in Santa Elena. With him he brought a plentitude of supplies from the Antilles and the Yucatan. There were live hogs and salt meat. There were tools for building and pikes and cords of wood for crossbows. There were cooking utensils and a big bronze bell to call the whole town together in case the French showed up.

Soon after arriving at Santa Elena, Menéndez scheduled a special meeting with Captain Juan Pardo. He confirmed to Pardo what was already evident to all: although provisions seemed good at the time, the poor land around Santa Elena could not sustain them, and the generosity of the local Indians and supplies from the Yucatan could not be counted on to keep everyone fed, what with Pardo's new additional 250 troops. Juan Pardo was ordered to take 125 troops and proceed inland on a multi-pronged mission, which must culminate in providing a reliable food supply for Santa Elena. He was to proceed up the rivers of the north to their headwaters at the base of the "Appalachee" Mountains. Then he must find the best route through the mountains and down over to the new silver mines in Zacatecas in New Spain, a distance which Menéndez calculated to be about 500 miles roundtrip.

Along the way of this route, Captain Pardo was to extend the hand of friendship to all local Indian rulers and convince them to relinquish sovereignty of their lands to the Spanish King, and sovereignty of their hearts to Jesus Christ and the Church of Rome. Also, along the way of this route to Zacatecas, Pardo was to establish a series of forts in prosperous Indian towns and require the chiefs there to keep a storehouse in each fort stocked with corn. In short, Juan Pardo was ordered to extend the Camino Real, the Royal Road, from its beginning in Mexico City to Santa Elena. Menéndez calculated that this task might take as long as seven months to achieve, and he assured Juan Pardo that he could do it and make a glorious name for himself.

Pardo asked, "Sir, why is it that, if we are looking for a route to the silver mines in Zacatecas which lies southwest of Santa Elena, you want me to follow Hernando de Soto's march northwest to encounter mountains which we would have to cross? Wouldn't it make sense to find a route straight to Mexico going south from here without crossing the Appalachee Mountains?"

"Pardo, yes, it would make sense to go southwest straight toward Zacatecas, if finding a road was our only goal. But de Soto confirmed, 26 years ago, that the land to the Southwest, between here and New Spain, had been depopulated due to Indian wars and the ravaging which he, himself, took part in. De Soto called it 'the wilderness of Ocute,' a vast area with no Indians, no towns, and no fields. Where are you going to find food in the wilderness of Ocute? Are you going to hunt and fish? Of course not. Not only for the survival of your men, but for Santa Elena itself and our plans to develop La Florida, you must go where the food is, along the rivers where all of the Indian tribes live.

"They are river people. They plant their corn and beans on the fertile flood plains along the rivers and creeks. Therefore, I ask of you, that in every village that has a Cacique you demand of the headman in the village that he build a storehouse to store corn for us. We must go where the natives are. They have built their towns in the best land, and we want to build our cities on that best land. And, besides that, to build new cities we need a workforce to build them and labor in the fields. If the Indians do not do this for us willingly, by paying taxes and supplying labor, then we will enslave them, or we will bring slaves in from Africa like we've had to do in Cuba, Hispaniola, and Puerto Rico. If the Indians don't cooperate we will make them third class subjects, irrelevant."

"I understand well, your Excellency. We will follow the rivers northwest where the people are and the food is grown," Juan Pardo responded.

"Yes, and one more thing. In every town that has the potential to become a Spanish City I want you to build a fort with a garrison to protect our interests. You know the French are our mortal enemies. I believe they are giving up their efforts to establish themselves in La Florida, but I think they are going to redouble their efforts at colonization to the north." Pointing to his map, Menéndez continued, "Follow the river that de Soto took to the northwest; the river he called 'Jordan River,' then after about 60 leagues from here, it turns to the west and proceeds to its headwaters at the mountains there. Take this route and cross the mountains at the headwaters of the Jordan. Build forts along the way. If the French come down from the north that line of forts will be our line of defense for La Florida."

"I will do so your Excellency."

"Good, so now you see that your mission cannot be more important. You are finding a road to Zacatecas to save our silver from the pirates; you are supplying us with food and a workforce, you will be founding the first Spanish cities of the interior of La Florida, and you will be protecting us from our enemies, the French. I addition to all this, you will become a very rich man, and your name will go down in history forevermore. For the next few months remain in Santa Elena and have your men continue to help Captain de Las Alas build the new fortifications and prepare you men to march north when the weather is cooler.

A month later, Menéndez revisited Santa Elena and was well-pleased with what Pardo and Las Alas had done. He ordered the fort expanded to accommodate a larger garrison and appointed Las Alas as Governor and Captain-General of Florida. He told Juan Pardo to prepare to leave in three months, by December 1566.

CHAPTER 3

THE TRAIL TO JOARA

DECEMBER 1566

Rumors of the impending expedition were circulating among the soldiers, whose number now included Ruy, Davide, Daniel, and Juan Martín de Badajoz, alias Juancinto Taranto. The four simply did not board the ship on its return voyage to Havana, and so, by default, they were now considered soldiers. As the rumor became fact, they were relieved to learn they would all be going together in the 125-man detachment which Captain Pardo was going to lead into the interior. In addition, their friend and tutor in the wild ways of the New World, Guillermo Rufín, would be going too as the principal interpreter for Captain Pardo.

The expedition left Santa Elena on the first of December, 1566, in a flotilla of canoes commandeered from the three closest Indian villages, Orista, Uscamacu, and Ahoya. The first night they spent in Orista, which allowed Rufín the opportunity to pass another night with Junica and bid farewell to her and his son. Daniel also managed to sneak off for a rendezvous with Sarati. To his surprise she had gained weight. Through body and sign language, she managed to communicate that she was pregnant, and he was to be the father.

Daniel, to his credit, took this news as fact. He showed neither shock or disbelief, but rather delight that he was to be part of a new creation. Their night together was tender and sleepless. He wondered how he was going to be the father that his father had been to him.

When Sarati awoke with the first light of day, he presented her with the gold chain with his mother's earring on it; the earring he had discovered covered in wax in a crack in the floorboards by the bed in the Captain's quarters of the *Redimido.*

The soldiers began to stir in the camp beside the village; cookfires lit with breakfast cooking. Daniel made his way into camp and ate with his comrades. They broke camp and began packing their goods in the canoes. Sarati appeared and kissed Daniel goodbye and then went over to Rufín and whispered something to him. He acknowledged the message and assured her that all would be all right. The canoes were launched and Daniel and Sarati gazed lovingly at each other as long as the lazy river allowed.

The expedition paddled all day until the river petered-out into a swamp at the village of Ahoya. Here they turned the canoes over to the Indians of the village and spent the night in the town center.

After eating, Rufín communicated to Daniel what Sarati had whispered in his ear. "She told me to tell you not to worry about how the child would be brought up."

"What did she mean by that?" Daniel asked.

"Well, in the first place, she is sure it is your child. And there will be no doubt after the birth. So, if you have doubts, you best keep them to yourself."

"I have no doubts," Daniel replied.

"Good. When she says for you not to worry, she means that she knows you are a warrior, and you may not ever find your way back to her, by death or circumstance. In your absence, the child, boy or girl, will have an uncle, Sarati's brother, Pamayato; the one who went on the spirit quest and who will be a medicine man. Pamayato will be the man in the child's life, responsible for safety and welfare. That is the way with their culture. It runs through the mother. If the father is not there, the mother's brother, the uncle, stands in. It goes without saying. The mother rules, and she can always be counted on to be there for the child. Not so with the father, who has many more ways to die. Sarati is telling you not to worry about the future of your child. If you don't return, the child will be brought up by the men and women of her family, and you will be still remembered and respected as the father."

Daniel replied, "This was quite unexpected news for me. Up until last night, I was only responsible for myself. Now I feel my world is changing, expanding, and at the same time shrinking."

Daniel Almeyda had now entered a strange new world, with a new family who did not even speak Portuguese or Spanish and with whom he did not live. Nothing seemed fixed and absolute, except for love. Even that was more like a business proposition. '*How strange,*' he thought.

"Daniel," Rufín offered, "if you try I will teach you the language of Orista so you can talk to your family."

"I'll make the effort," replied Daniel.

"Good, but I'll warn you, I'm not the hotshot interpreter that Menéndez and Pardo think I am. I only know Orista well, and that is one of the hundreds of dialects, and I'm just talking about the tribes along the coast. I don't know how I'm going to deal with the Caciques to the north, but we'll find out."

"Great Rufín, I'll take you up on that. You teach me Orista, and I will teach you Arabic."

"Arabic?" Rufín countered in surprise. "Oh yes, you did tell me about Ceuta on the coast of Morocco. I guess you do speak Arabic. But I'll pass on that, thank you. I don't think there'll be much use for Arabic over here. If you're serious about learning languages we'll have our hands full just learning Catawban, Cherokee, and Yucchi, but particularly Catawban, because in a week or so that's all we are going to hear."

"Okay. You teach me the language of Orista, and we will both study the Catawba tongue."

"Agreed." finalized Rufín.

The next morning the real journey began—no more canoes. No horses or donkeys and no captured Indian slaves like de Soto had resorted to. 125 soldiers carried all their provisions on their backs, with most of the weight in building and trade articles like shovels, axe heads, wedges, nails, lead shot, gunpowder, cloth, beads, and trinkets. They were thankful that it was early December, which meant that vegetation in the swamps and sandhills was at a minimum, and the heat and humidity were tolerable. They had Indian guides who kept them on the right path toward each daily destination. Most trails coincided with the river and creek banks. A few trails moved laterally from one river basin to another. At times they would follow a path through a swampy creek that had been a river. There were alligators and snakes in the swamps, but the march made such a racket that these demons were generally scared away.

The first night they camped at the village of Ahoyabe. The second night they reached Cocao. There they noted that the soil was notably improved, changing from sandy to more of red clay with stones. They were rising in elevation, and the creeks and rivers were running faster with sweeter water. Juan Pardo saw that the land was suitable for all the crops necessary to sustain a Spanish population. From Cacao, they marched north and in two days reached the village of Aboyaca on the bank of a large river. From here, they turned northeast along a trail through dense swamps and, after two days, reached a large town at the union of two big rivers. The town was called Guiomae, and it was perched along the west bank of the river that de Soto had called Jordan, but was generally referred to as Catawba River, in reference to the Indian tribe that lived along its banks.

The soldiers were now 130 miles, or 40 leagues, from Santa Elena. Pardo began to record all events as Menéndez had ordered. This was in accordance with strict Spanish bureaucracy, which specified that anything happening within 40 leagues of a Capital, was within the authority of that Capital, in this case, Santa Elena, and therefore, technically, not Pardo's responsibility to record or to treat as a problem.

Juan Pardo recalled from the archives that Guiomae was the place that de Soto had reached 40 years previously after spending a week with his army crossing the wilderness of Ocute to the south and without seeing hardly an Indian. As de Soto approached Guiomae, he had desperately looked for a fabulously wealthy city, the legendary golden city the tribes had first told him about hundreds of miles to the south. The chief of this mighty city was said to be a woman. It was here in Guiomae that de Soto took hostages and tortured them, trying to make them tell the location of the famous city, which he heard was called Confitachequi. Those he seized and tortured committed suicide rather than reveal to de Soto that "Confitachequi or Canos" as it was also called, lay only two days march up the big river. Pardo could see that this land had some promise. The terrain not covered in swamp was fertile, and the location was good with access to two rivers, which converged leading to the sea.

When the Pardo expedition arrived in Guiomae his men were greeted by a few hundred people, including many Caciques from villages nearby and distant. The Cacique of Guiomae was named Emae Orata. From Rufín, Pardo understood that the various Caciques were aware of Pardo's march from Santa Elena and had congregated here expecting

Pardo to arrive. At this time, Juan Pardo assembled a group of soldiers, including Villamar, his ensign, and Juan de la Bandera, the official notary, archivist, and accountant. He then summoned Guillermo Rufín to translate for an official ceremony.

Davide was nearby and he overheard the oath that Rufín swore. Rufín had to swear by the sign of the cross and Holy Mary that as the official interpreter of the expedition, and the one who understood the Indian languages, that he would always tell the truth about everything that would be treated and agreed upon between the Indians and this expedition, so that an extensive report could be given to His Majesty and the document would be accurate. Furthermore, Rufín conceded to the fact that if he kept to his oath, God would aid him in this world in his body, and in the next world his soul would endure longer. However, if he should lie, or not honor his oath, the opposite should occur.

Rufín swore to do this with an "Amen" and signed his name to the notary's document.

At this point, Pardo requested Emae Orata, the Head Chief of Guiomae, to assemble all the various Caciques who had gathered there to witness a demonstration of his harquebuse rifles and the lead ball projecting crossbows. After the assemblage was duly impressed, Pardo gave the first of his many standard speeches for which he was obliged by Adelantado Menéndez. Rufín translated from Spanish into his Orista tongue, hoping the Caciques would understand.

Juan Pardo stated to the Indians that he had come in friendship to take dominion of the land in the name of the King of Spain and the Pope of the Catholic Church. They were now all subjects of King Phillip of Spain and Pope Pius V in Rome. In order to feed the Spanish soldiers who would periodically be in Guiomae, the natives were to build a storehouse and fill it with corn. All the households of the land around Guiomae were to carry a quantity of corn each year to the storehouse. If they did not have corn, they could bring deerskins, and if they did not have deerskins, they could bring salt. The storehouse would belong to the King, and no one was to remove anything from the storehouse without permission from the King. Pardo then said that if they would like to become Christians, he would have monks sent to their villages to teach them the catechism.

After Rufín translated this into Orista and into what little he had learned of the Catawban language, the Captain handed out gifts of axe heads, chisels, and knives to the Caciques and other important men who had gathered, and they all gladly accepted the gifts. Then Pardo asked the assembled Caciques if they would like to formally give possession of their land to His Majesty. They all responded with a resounding "Yaa," which Rufín, and the Spanish took to be, "yes." Next, Juan de la Bandera, along with Rufín, secured the name of each Cacique present, and Bandera wrote it in an official document.

The following days brought them to the villages of Canos, some of which had mounds with council houses on top. By afternoon they reached the principal town of Talimeco where there were four larger mounds.

In earlier times, Canos or Confitachequi, had been the Paramount Chiefdom for hundreds of miles in all directions, but even at the time of Hernando de Soto, 26 years before, Canos had been long past its prime. It had become decimated by smallpox and the loss of power and prestige at the hands of far-flung enemies, such as the chiefdom of Coosa two hundred miles to the west. When de Soto first entered Cano's principal temple town of Talimeco, he had expeceted to see another Inca or Aztec capital. What he found was uncut grass growing in the streets and dilapidation of the ceremonial ancestor-worshiping houses near the Temple Mounds surrounded by corpses piled high and marked by smallpox. The famous "Lady of Confitachequi" had fled into the swamps and sent out her niece, carried on a litter, to meet de Soto and his men.

De Soto and his army of 600 Spaniards and 1500 Indian mercenaries had stayed for a few weeks looting the temples. The ultimate treasure here was river pearls, not gold or silver. De Soto took a prisoner and tortured him to reveal the whereabouts of their queen, but the man then punctured his own chest with an arrow to avoid disclosing his queen's hiding place. After ravaging all the food, de Soto took the niece of the Chieftess as a hostage and began a march north up along the bank of the River Jordan.

If Canos had been in decline at the time of de Soto, now, in the day of Juan Pardo, it had reached decimation. In de Soto's day, there were little more than two paramount Chiefdoms in all the Southeast of the continent—Confitachequi and Coosa. The paramount Chief, or Great Lord, ruled over dozens, if not hundreds of simple chiefdoms. The larger chiefdoms were governed by Micos, and the smaller ones were governed by Oratas. When Juan Pardo arrived in 1566, Confitachequi was not even governed by a Mico, but only by an Orata who was little more than the sheriff of a small town, but it was still a place with history and prestige. If Confitachequi was on the decline at the time of de Soto, another Chiefdom, also visited by de Soto and far up the so called Jordan River, was on the ascent. This was the Chiefdom of Joara, and Joara was Captain Pardo's prime destination.

Despite the apparent decline of Canos, Juan Pardo could easily visualize a future Spanish city on the site of Canos. The town was situated just above the fall line of the great river, where the flat coastal soil gave way to the hilly, red, and rocky soil, ideal for crops and grapes and still suitable for river navigation.

Although Canos was impoverished, it was still centrally located for many of the villages and small chiefdoms which had always paid tribute to it. Therefore, when Juan Pardo arrived, there were over 30 Caciques waiting for him. He and Rufín gave the same formal speech that was delivered in Guiomae two days before, and all the Oratas said "yaa."

Later that night, David and Ruy asked Rufín about how he felt about having to translate the Captain's speeches ordering the people to change their lives, and about how he felt about his oath in front of the notary he took two days ago. Rufín looked at them as if they were dullards. After some moments of silence, he asked them, "Did you hear what happened last year when my godfather Captain-General Jean Ribault, and the French fleet arrived at the same time and place on the coast of Florida as the Spanish Captain-General Pedro Menéndez with his warships?"

Davide replied, "We heard about it, but no one could give us the details."

"Well I will tell you, then, and destroy your ignorance," Rufín stated.

"As I told Ruy and Daniel last summer on our canoe trip to Orista, the French Captain Jean Ribault more or less adopted me when my parents were killed. He signed me up as cabin boy on the first voyage to Santa Elena four years ago. When Charlesfort collapsed I went to live with the Oristas where the Spanish found me and took me to Havana. Two years ago, the French and Jean Ribault Ribault came back and built a substantial fort on an island in the inlet of the Saint John's River about 12 leagues north of San Augustín, a perfect location to threaten the Spanish treasure ships coming up from New Spain.

"When Pedro Menéndez, in Spain, heard that Ribault had built Fort Caroline, in the Saint John's River, he was furious. He set out from Cádiz with several ships and a thousand soldiers to destroy the fort. At about the same time, Jean Ribault set out from France with several ships, supplies, and reinforcements for the new colony at Fort Caroline. Ribault arrived on the coast of Florida two weeks before Menéndez, because Menéndez's fleet had encountered a hurricane in the middle of the Ocean Sea. When Menéndez arrived on the coast near San Augustín, he sailed north along the beach until he saw Ribault's fleet anchored at the island at the mouth of Saint John's River. Menéndez approached the French fleet and fired a few shots and then quickly withdrew. The Spanish fleet sailed down the coast looking for the first good inlet and found one where San Augustín is now. Of course, the fort was not there yet. Menéndez claimed the land of San Augustín for Spain.

"Ribault, believing the Spanish were retreating due to his superior strength, took after them with his four ships, all his artillery, and six hundred men. He left only a small garrison to protect Fort Caroline. Ribault was hoping this would be the final showdown between the French and Spanish in La Florida.

"Ribault's fleet was sailing south along the coast in pursuit of Menéndez when a thunderstorm arose just as they were passing the inlet to San Augustín. Because of the storm they did not see the inlet or the Spanish fleet waiting for them. Ribault kept sailing down the coast looking for Menéndez, but before it was evident that he had gone too far, his fleet sailed into the path of a hurricane. It wrecked his ships and divided his army into two parties, each stranded separately on La Florida's beaches.

"Menéndez, meanwhile, after seeing the French fleet sail by with so many men aboard its ships, figured that the garrison at Fort Caroline must be poorly defended. He left some soldiers at San Augustín and then led five hundred soldiers for two days along the beach and through the marshes to Fort Caroline. They overran the fort at night with no trouble and killed 132 men, sparing only the women and children.

"After seizing Fort Caroline, Menéndez changed the name to Fort San Mateo. Later, he returned to San Augustín to protect his position there and wait for the French ships. After waiting for a couple of weeks, Menéndez learned from local Indians that one group of French shipwreck survivors had congregated on a beach about five leagues south of San Augustín. Menéndez marched to meet them. The French soldiers were, of course, desperate, and immediately surrendered, but Menéndez killed them all without mercy. Soon after that, Jean Ribault and the other party of shipwrecked French soldiers arrived at that same beach, which is now called Matanzas. They were starving and looking for their comrades. Menéndez put them all to the sword, including Captain-General Jean Ribault, my godfather.

"Now, I serve at the pleasure of Captain-General Menéndez as an official interpreter. When the Adelantado in Havana first interviewed me, the first thing Menéndez asked me was, not if I were French, because, of course, he knew that, but, if I was a Catholic. I told him, "yes," that I had been raised a Catholic. Thank God he believed me! He said that after my ordeal with the Indians, he did not exactly regard me as a Frenchman, which was good because the only thing he hated more than a Frenchman as a demonic French Protestant Huguenot, who, with the help of Lucifer, worked against the Pope and the Church of God.

"So, what I am telling you is that Menéndez did not leave a single Frenchman on the coast of La Florida alive, believing that they might be Huguenots. So why would I tell him that I was a Huguenot? He believes because of the storms and hurricanes that he has God on his side, that the slaughter of the Huguenots was a righteous act, and that with God on his side he can do no wrong. Who am I to defy him? And you two, if you tell the Adelantado that I am a Huguenot, I will kill you if he does not kill me first. Anyway, I will tell him that you all are not only Portuguese spies, but you secretly practice your religion and blasphemy Jesus Christ and the Holy Virgin. Is that clear?"

Davide said calmly, "Relax Rufín. As you know, we are not spying, nor do we openly practice our religion. We are running from persecution, just like the Huguenots in France. We admire and look up to you and want to learn from you and be like you. We would never betray you just as we know that you would never betray us."

Ruy added, "Yes, for us, you are a model of survival. We call you *um bocado da cortica no mar,*" a piece of cork on the sea. A survivor. And we want to be corks and survivors like you."

"All right. I believe you," Rufín sighed, before he was reminded of one more strange thing about the Huguenots that Menéndez said, which made him laugh.

"One day," Rufín began, "Menéndez asked me what I knew about the Apalachee Mountains and what lay beyond to the west. I told him that I did not know anything first-hand about that, but that my people said that there was a very great river that ran from north to south many days beyond the mountains. He asked me if I had ever heard of a tribe called the Chichimecas?

Rufín stopped and looked at Davide and Ruy and asked, "Have you ever heard of the Chichimecas?"

They told him, "No."

"That's what I told the Adelantado exactly. He said that the Chichimecas were a very large, unruly tribe that was harassing the silver mines at San Martín and Zacatecas in New Spain. The Chichimeca came down from the north and would not accept the Catholic Church and the rule of Spain. Menéndez thinks that the Chichimeca tribe inhabits the land just beyond the Appalachee Mountains. He expressed to me that he had a fear that the French Huguenots were like the Chichimecas. He was afraid that the Huguenots would find the road to Zacatecas before he did. Then the Huguenots, being pagan, would ally with the Chichimecas and become a formidable army and seize the silver mines. That is why he had to kill all the Huguenots—because they might link up with the Chichimecas! What do you think about that?"

Both Davide and Ruy shrugged their shoulders, pulled at their beards, and wondered what a strange world they were entering.

When the expedition left Canos, it proceeded up the east bank of the River Jordan, which Rufín referred to as the Catawba River after the name the indigenous people called their nation.

Marching up the river trail at the end of each day, they would arrive at a Catawba town. Captain Pardo would give his formal speech to the assembled Caciques from the neighboring villages, and Rufín would translate into crude Catawban. Again, the Chiefs would give affirmation to Pardo's presentation with a resounding "Yaa."

The men marched up the river trail for six days and camped overnight in six towns where the local Caciques heard the same speech, were given axe heads, steel knives, and acquiesced without protest to the idea of building corn cribs to store food for the Spanish.

It was approaching Christmas Day when the small army, now marching west instead of northwest along the north bank of the Catawba River, arrived at the confluence of a small hardy river coming down from the north. The river was full of canoe traffic, which offered to transport Pardo's men across. The canoe paddlers indicated that Joara was just up the tributary. Some of the soldiers wanted Captain Pardo to insist that the Indians in their canoes transport them up to Joara to lessen the journey and the burden on their tired backs, but the Catawban guide was against this, saying that following the track, they would soon come to a creek that would lead directly to Joara. It was only a league or two away. Soon enough, they were traveling up that creek, which Rufín translated from the Catawban as "Warrior Creek."

Every mile or so up Warrior Creek, there was a village on one side of the water or the other. At each village, the population, led by a head man, would come out to greet the Spanish parade, and the villagers would accompany the soldiers with singing and dancing through their village and on to the next. After passing through six or seven of these villages, they came to a place where Warrior Creek was joined by another creek. There the forest opened to a broad floodplain, an elongated valley surrounded by hills bearing healthy deciduous trees, leafless in the late December air. By now, over one thousand dancing or otherwise curious souls were accompanying Juan Pardo's party of 125 men. On a large boulder where the creeks converged sat Tacoru, known as Joara Mico, the paramount Chief and lord of the region. The news of Pardo's march to Joara had long preceded his arrival. Joara Mico was over 60 years old but still a powerful man. Pardo, with his steel helmet, breastplate, chainmail, tall boots, and sword, saw Joara Mico, dressed in painted deerskin britches, a shirt, a bearskin shawl, and a headdress of turkey feathers. They formally met, and both Pardo and Joara Mico were then carried on litters through the central village of about 100 thatched-doomed white wattle structures and then over to the Ceremonial Mound, 40 yards in diameter and 20 feet high, upon which sat the square council house.

Joara Mico and Juan Pardo, with his interpreter, Rufín, mounted the steps to the top of the Sacred Mound. Standing outside the council house, Juan Pardo gazed over the settlement and thought, '*how different this place is from Canos, barely alive in its decline with dozens of overgrown mounds and sad citizens trapped in the glory and ceremony of times gone bye. Joara is a place on the rise with its people joyous and industrious.*'

He looked out over the valley and could see hectares after hectares of fields with corn stubble and corncribs, while the hills surrounding the valley would be perfect for grapes. The beauty of Joara's natural setting reminded him of his hometown of Cuenca, east of Madrid. He liked the feel of this place. He told himself that this would be his city. Then he looked to the horizon from his vantage place on top the mound, past the surrounding hills with their leafless trees, into the western distance and caught his first glimpse of the fabled Appalachee Mountains. There, atop a hazy blue mountain in the late afternoon, was something gleaming like a diamond; sunlight was bouncing off a cap of snow on the distant mountain range in the clear, crisp air. Captain Pardo, who was rarely in a hurry, thought to himself, '*how near we are. But snow! I can't take my men over those mountains covered in snow with no food supply. We will wait here, east of the mountains, until spring, and in the meantime build forts and storehouses for the corn. Then we will find a road to Zacatecas on the other side of those mountains.*'

Using Ruffin to translate, Captain Pardo praised the land of Joara to the Great Chief, and then asked the Chief if there were other Caciques here at this time that would like to hear the speech that he wanted to deliver? Joara Mico told him that more than 20 Caciques were present, coming from near and distant villages and that he would summons them and bring them to the council house.

Many thoughts and memories ran through Tacoru's mind. '*It has been many years since I've seen a man dressed like Juan Pardo.*' He had been a young warrior in line to succeed his father as Orata of Joara. Just as now, the word had come up the river from Confitachequi that an army of strange men was advancing, riding on the backs of huge animals. Their leader was named Soto, and following his army, were a thousand Indian warriors from the far south employed to fight for Soto. When they marched up the river and creeks, and entered the valley of Joara, they filled the whole valley. The day after Soto arrived Joara Orata, fearing the worst, sent his sisters away to a remote village. Tacoru continued to reminisce:

'The army ate everything and took all the corn from the corn cribs. Soto himself shot a lead ball out of a stick with a piece of fire, but the worst were their war dogs. They were larger and more vicious than wolves. The local people were in awe as Soto showed them how fast, once released, the war dogs could run down, kill, and begin to eat a man, tearing apart his limbs and members. We were no match for Soto,' Tacoru thought, *'so we kept our distance and gave him food. Soon he was gone. I see that this group of Spanish soldiers is much smaller, no horses, no herds of pigs, and no army of Timucan warriors ready to do their bidding. I only see one soldier with a war dog on a leash.'.*

On his march, Soto killed many people, took slaves, food, and spread disease. He marched in here, so proud of his hostage, the noble niece of the Queen of Canos. When he left here and marched into the mountains, Coosa Mico and Tuscaloosa gathered the Caciques and tribes and stood up against him. They fought for many, many moons until they wore Soto out, and then they killed him. Joara Mico thought to himself, *'now he is just a bad memory. Joara survived and prospered. I will handle this Pardo in the same way my father handled Soto. I will accept his terms and graciously accept any useful gifts he has to offer. Soon enough, he too will be gone, a fading memory.'*

Joara Mico called the various Caciques, and they congregated at the base of the mound. Captain Pardo, with Rufín at his side, came halfway down the log steps and addressed the sub-chiefs assembled below. Pardo informed them that the land was now under the domain of the King of Spain, the most Paramount Chief in the world. They must submit and give an oath of allegiance to His Majesty King Phillip. If they were to survive in this new Dominion, they should submit their hearts and souls to Jesus Christ and follow the dictates of His Church as headed by the Pope. If they would like to do this, then they would be supplied with monks to teach them the cateclysm. As a testament to their loyalty, they must all build corncribs and storehouses in their villages to supply food for the Spanish rulers. All the Caciques agreed to do this, and they affirmed their will by pronouncing the word "yaa." Juan Pardo then handed out axe heads, wedges, chisels, and knives along with colored cloth and trinkets to the Caciques, and each one seemed content.

CHAPTER 4

FORT SAN JUAN

JOARA
JANUARY – JUNE 1567

Looking out from the mound toward the western mountains, Juan Pardo barely noticed the dwellings to his left spread out along the L-shaped bend of Warrior Creek. He did not see the columns of late afternoon cookfire smoke rising to the clouds in all directions. He rather saw, in his mind's eye, rows of cobblestone streets between white plastered buildings all converging on a central square with a Cathedral and a belfry tolling out the hours. This place, with rivers and creeks streaming through it, with fertile fields surrounded by rolling hills leading to the mountains reminded him of his beloved home where he grew up, the city of Cuenca. That's it. He would name this new city of his imagination "Cuenca," and the fort he was first going to build, starting tomorrow, would be named after his namesake saint, San Juan.

That night in his tent, by lantern light, with his ensign, Villamar, and Sergeant Moyano, Juan Pardo drew on parchment the design for Fort San Juan. The dimensions were 40 feet wide by 60 feet long, built with outer rectangle logs 12 feet high. Pardo also planned for a dry moat surrounding the fort, eight feet wide and seven feet deep. Within the walls, the sawed wood-plank structure would be of a single story, except for a two-story room in the middle for storing the treasured items such as gun powder, match cord, lead, axe heads, chisels, knives, and other trade goods. The design of the second-floor arsenal included sleeping quarters for the officers. He would place the fort beside the creek and upstream from the earthen mound with the Joara Council House. After all, there were reasons the wise Indians had placed the mound where it was, and whatever those reasons were he was going to take advantage of them.

The next day was a frenzy of activity with teams of Spaniards and Indians going into the forests to fell trees. The Spaniards taught the Indians how to use the iron axe, and teams of Indians would pull the logs into the town center, where a crude muscle-driven sawmill was set-up. Boundary logs were cut to the same length, and other logs were sawed into planks for the walls, the roof, and the floors. Along the fort boundary line, using metal picks and shovels, soldiers and Indians dug a two-foot deep trench into which the boundary logs were erected, side-by-side. Perched on newly made ladders, a team of burley Spaniards were positioned atop the wall as it went forth. The team struggled with a 50 pound boulder, which they used to hammer each log of the advancing wall firmly into the trench.

As the boundary wall was being built, another large crew on the outside was digging the moat. The dirt from the moat was brought into the emerging fort to raise the floor level inside. Still another crew, using four-inch iron nails, hammered the wood planks for the fort structure in place as soon as the sawmill could produce them. In four days the fort was finished, which was, for the indigenous population of Joara, a marvel to behold.

Joara Mico could not help but be impressed by the organization, discipline, tools, and craftsmanship of the Spaniards. He had already seen a display, 20 years ago, of the deadly crossbow, the armor, mail-cloth, and swords of steel. To resist the Spaniards would be pointless, if not deadly stupid. And, when Joara Mico reflected upon the past, he could not deny that since the days when de Soto passed through, the Chiefdom of his father, and now his own, had grown in power and prestige.

Joara now rivaled and even surpassed, the once-great Canos to the south, and to the east the Guatari with women as chiefs was not much of a rival. Joara's power and reputation almost matched that of Coosa in the far southwest. His only problem now was with the Chisca in the north, that strange tribe which thought they controlled the trade in salt, mica, and copper—all the gems of Mother Earth.

In defiance of the Chisca, Joara Mico had developed his own source of salt from boiling the water coming from three springs at the base of the nearby mountain. He was taking business away from Chisca Mico now, and the Chiscan war chief did not like it. He had already threatened a war party against the Joaran salt traders. *'Perhaps the power and awe of the Spaniards,'* Joara Mico thought, *'can be used to advance Joara over Chisca, while the Spaniards are still here.'* This will be the best course of action, he paused, *'after all, Joara will be here long after this Juan Pardo is gone.'*

Spectacular progress was made that first week. The work crews of Spaniards and Indians had gotten along well with the building of the fort, and more than that, the week had been like a celebration. Juan Pardo felt that the people of Joara were truly glad that he and his men had arrived. Each night the Spaniards and those Indians who had worked were treated to all they could consume of bear meat stew. This was a rare delight in January, as the bears were hibernating in their hiding places at the foot of the mountains to the north and west. But the hunters had found a cave with a bear couple and their cub sleeping.

By that evening, their meat was stewing in large caldrons by the mound, and their skins were stretched out on a hill where a group of crows was picking away at the last morsels. That night snow fell, and all of Pardo's men wished they were curled up in a bear-skin blanket like those drying out on the nearby hill.

The building of the fort had gone so well that Captain Pardo authorized the construction of two barracks, both with dimensions of 25 feet by 25 feet. These barracks were built outside the walled fort. Pardo reasoned he would leave 20 men in Joara, ten men in each barrack.

Pardo marveled at the fact that, without his input or order, the essential activity of food production was being handled by old and young women from the surrounding villages or neighborhoods, that is, by matrons well past their prime, and young women barely past puberty.

The married women of Joara were at home, out of harm's way, with their children and chores while many of their husbands were out hunting to support the community and their newly arrived guests.

After the bear meat was consumed, the following days saw the garrison settle into a more routine diet of venison and turkey, with corn mush, beans, squash, and soups with a paste of acorn, hickory, and other nuts. Drinking water was taken upstream from Warrior Creek which ran less than 100 feet to the east of the fort. Captain Pardo thought about digging a well, but until such time that it was dug, creek water would be boiled for his men's consumption.

After two weeks, and as the first of the barracks was being completed, Juan Pardo announced that he was going to visit the powerful Chiefdom to the east called Guatari. This was another large population center like Joara and was located on another high-volume river called Yadkin. This Yadkin River, like the Catawba or Jordan River, flowed east to the sea with headwaters in the western mountains. And like the Catawba, the Yadkin River started with an easterly flow and turned south toward Santa Elena and the coast. The Micos of Guatari sent representatives to meet the Spanish expedition in Canos. It would have been closer for the Micos to have come to Joara to meet Captain Pardo, but as they explained to Rufín, Guatari and Joara were not on good terms, so they did not want to venture into Joara.

In fact, the territory of Guatarí was headed by two women, one young and the other older. When these Mico women heard about the story of Jesus Christ, the Lord, and Savior, they very much wanted Juan Pardo to send a monk to teach them the catechism. Indeed, Juan Pardo had such a monk, Father Sebastian Montero, who was traveling with the expedition with the purpose of Christianizing the populace. Joara Mico had requested to Juan Pardo that the monk stay in Joara to teach them, but something told Pardo not to leave Father Montero in Joara, but to honor the prior request and take the monk to Guatarí.

Captain Pardo departed Joara with 95 of his men and followed the trail beside the Catawba River for four days. The path ran east by northeast until the river turned south, at which point they departed from the that river and journeyed on the trading trail east across the country until they came to Guatari on the bank of the Yadkin River. Juan Pardo was well received by both the old and the young Chieftess of Guatari, and he quickly got to work building a fort larger than the one he had left in Joara. This structure had the dual purpose of serving as both a fort and a mission. During the construction of the Guatari Fort, Juan Pardo received a message by way of a runner from Captain-General de las Alas in Santa Elena, saying that Pardo's presence was urgently needed in Santa Elena because there was an imminent threat of a French attack on the city.

Needing as many men as possible to face the French threat, Juan Pardo left in Guatarí only 4 soldiers along with Father Sebastian Montero. The Captain then proceeded with the remaining 90 men down the trail beside the Yadkin River and then traveled west over to the Catawba and down this river past Canos and Guiomae and over to Ahoyabe, one day's journey from Orista, and from there a canoe ride to Santa Elena.

On March 7, 1567, Pardo and 90 soldiers pulled up at the dock in Santa Elena with 24 canoes supplied by Orista Orata. The French never did show up to avenge the massacre of the previous year by Pedro Menéndez. The Adelantado did, however, visit Santa Elena shortly after Juan Pardo returned. Menéndez was pleased to hear about the progress that Juan Pardo had made during the four months of his expedition. He was particularly interested in Pardo's description of Guatarí, with its fertile hills and its full-flowing river that ran all the way to the coast. Inspired by this description, Menéndez began to make plans to locate his personal estate at Guatarí and build his empire out from and around the town. But the royal road to Zacatecas was yet to be discovered. He ordered Juan Pardo back on the trail with 125 men.

The Adelantado told Captain Pardo that, this time, he was not to dawdle in Joara but cross through the Appalachee Mountains and proceed directly to the silver mines in Zacatecas. He even gave Pardo explicit instructions about just what to do as his expedition approached the jurisdiction of Zacatecas and San Miguel, so as not to create surprise and distress among the monks. The message for the mission in Zacatecas included an order for the bishop to send monks to the forts that Pardo had built and to send word by boat to Havana of the success of the expedition.

Captain Pardo, perhaps not wanting to march through the lowland swamps in mid-summer, spent time through the hot season resupplying and mobilizing for the second expedition. On September 1, 1567, he set out on the same trail he took ten months earlier to Joara.

For the eight months of Captain Juan Pardo's absence from Joara, Sergeant Hernando Moyano had been left in charge of the new garrison. Moyano was frequently seen strutting around Pardo's "Cuenca" with his Irish war dog on a leash as he gave orders. Periodically, he would call for an hour of target practice to demonstrate the awesome power of his fire shooting harquebus and crossbows that shot lead slugs. The warriors of Joara were always impressed. They did, however, notice that a weakness of the harquebus, whose secret powder was applied like a medicine and was then ignited with a burning matchlock cord. They noted that the matchlock fuse would not burn when exposed to rain, so the secret powder was ineffective in bad weather. Likewise, the crossbow and its lead projectile could easily kill a man at a short distance and could be rapidly reloaded, but the crossbow archers were not particularly accurate, and certainly could not be compared with a good Catawba bowman.

Daniel, who proved to be a reasonably good marksman with the harquebus was allowed to accompany a Joaran hunting party looking for bear and dear. He demonstrated his prowess and brought back to the kitchen the carcasses of a stag and a doe. He claimed the skins and had an outfit made for himself.

Working to construct the fort and the two barracks was the most laborious work Davide and Ruy had ever done, and that was probably also true of Daniel. After the ocean voyage and months of mediocre food at Santa Elena, followed by a month of marching through swamps and along riverbank trails, the three Portuguese with the Spanish Gypsy were finally eating and sleeping well. Once a week, bear meat would be served instead of deer or turkey, and they came to love to the taste. As week followed week, they grew stronger from the hard work and good meat, balanced with corn mush, squash, and beans with soups of acorn and hickory nuts.

Joara was a trading center where a few different languages and many dialects met. It was a natural crossroad between two major trading trails. One trail starting in the northeast ran through Virginia to the Occoneechee trading island in the Roanoke River. That trail continued west through Joara and into the mountains of the Cherokee. From there the trading trail turned south through the Creek Chiefdom of Coosa. The other primary path was the one that de Soto and Juan Pardo had taken up from the southeastern coast, then following the Catawba River north to Joara. This great path, after crossing the east-west trading path at Joara, went northwest up through the mountains following the Nolichucky River past the land of the Chisca and out beyond the Appalachee Range and into the great valleys where big rivers run. Following this trading path north along the rivers leads to the place where salt was mined and traded throughout the vast region.

Rufín's initial stay in Joara lasted only two weeks. He then accompanied Pardo, as his interpreter, to Guatarí and then south, back to Santa Elena. During his short time in Joara, Rufín attracted the attention of a young man by the name of Erbani, the son of Pantanhaya, the principle medicine man of Joara. Erbani wanted to learn the language of the Conquistadors. The Frenchman agreed to teach him, and in return Erbani would give Rufín instruction in Catawban and other various languages spoken in Joara.

Rufín arranged to meet in the evenings at the house Erbani shared with his parents and twin sister, Vara. When it became evident that Rufín would be leaving soon after beginning his class with Erbani, Guillermo suggested that two of his friends, Ruy and Davide, take his place. This was agreed upon, and after a few evenings working with Erbani, Ruy asked if Daniel and Juan Martín de Badajoz might also join the group. This was permitted, and Vara, Erbani's twin sister, consented to participate helping her brother, now with a class of four.

During the day Erbani usually worked in the family fields of corn, squash, beans, and the herb garden that grew by the San Juan River. This little river newly christened by Juan Pardo for his patron Saint, was located only a half-mile east of Fort San Juan and paralleled Warrior Creek for ten miles going south before emptying into the Catawba River.

Vara, too, spent much of her time in the family fields beside the San Juan River. She oversaw tending the extensive family medicinal and herb garden, upon which her father, as the medicine man, relied. She often went with her father into the forest to hunt medicinal herbs, and once she even went with Pantanhaya on a three-day trip west up into the Wild Gorge by Table Rock to find a rare herb to cure her mother's double vision.

Soon, after embarking on the nightly language lessons, Davide and Vara discovered they had an affinity for each other. Of the four exiles from Iberia, Davide, the youngest and least experienced, tended to be the one who worried the most. Vara's cheerful eyes and natural smile, combined with her soft but firm rhythmic voice had a calming effect on anyone in her presence, especially Davide. Although he could understand only a little of what she said, the sound of her words acted as a lullaby for his young soul. Physically, Vara was on the small side, feminine but strong and very healthy. Her round face and large dark eyes reminded Davide of a Portuguese doll. And this, in some strange way, relieved Davide of his "*saudage*," tying him back to a secure and enchanted childhood.

One morning, Davide, while working on building Barracks Number Two, observed Vara delivering a basket of fresh bear meat to the hearth of the Spanish kitchen. Davide stopped working and walked over to the kitchen to practice greeting her in Catawban. She returned the greeting in Spanish to the concern of the Indian matrons tending the cook fire, who noticed her flirting eyes. Davide learned that Vara, through her father, had managed to be assigned to the cooking detail to serve the visiting Spanish. To Davide, this meant that he could see her both during the day and at night, and perhaps even eat better.

After a week of serving on kitchen detail, Vara decided to talk to her best friend, Xequina, and ask her to join this daily routine. Xequina was the daughter of the Orata of the nearby village, just a half-mile up the Warrior Creek. The idea appealed to Xequina, and she pressured her father until she finally convinced him to allow her to seek work at the Spanish barrack's kitchen, preparing food each day for the soldiers.

Xequina, like Vara, was 16 years old, but there the similarities stopped. Xequina was already an imposing figure. She was as tall as most of the Spanish soldiers. She had long, graceful legs, arms and fingers, and a short, slender torso with an elegant neck supporting a head surrounded by an aura of curly black hair. There was a wild beauty about her with her perfectly formed lips and radiant smile, but her most defining feature were the eyes. They were naturally not as cheerful as Vara's, but more probing. Without a moment's notice, her eyes could switch from gleeful mirth to hot intensity that could burn a hole in Juan Pardo's steel helmet. Xequina's father, Routau, was the head of the family clan and his village. Although a neighborhood "headman," Routan's authority was no match against his daughter's will whenever she set her mind toward something. And so, it was that Vara and Xequina gained permission to work every day in the open-air-kitchen at the plaza by the barracks and fort.

The girls both wore deerskin leggings along with deerskin tops and moccasins. Vara had told Xequina of the nightly visits to her house with Rufín for language study with her brother, and with the departure of Rufín, now Davide, Ruy, Daniel, and Juan Martín were coming to her house to study with Erbani. Xequina was eager that she, too, be a part of this group, but she knew that her father would not let her out of the house after sundown; therefore, she had to make the most of her days.

On the morning that Vara and Xequina first arrived in the plaza for kitchen duty, Ruy could not take his eyes off the tall girl. The maidens of Orista in one long night, with their sweet voices and soothing touch, had helped him to quell any feeling of guilt he might have had about being unfaithful to the memory of Ana Sophia. Indeed, after seeing Xequina for the first time, swaying about the kitchen fire, he experienced heartfelt appreciation for the maidens of Orista. His vitality and desires now restored, Ruy approached Xequina with his best try at a Catawban morning greeting, and she coquettishly responded with a giggling, "*Buenos Dias*." He later caught her staring at him, or was it the reverse— she caught him? In any case, they looked away and smiled.

Davide and Vara naturally took to one another. When occasion allowed at mealtimes, Davide would chat with Vara to improve communication skills. One morning, Davide suffered a large splinter in his hand while sawing planks for the interior walls of Barracks Number One. After the big lunch that Vara had helped prepare, she removed the splinter with a chicken bone needle. Then, while the others were having their siesta, Vara led Davide down the long path to her medicinal garden over by the little San Juan River. She was looking for the plant, lamb's quarters, to make a poultice so Davide's wound would not be infected.

On the 20 minute walk to the river, east of the town center, they were caught by a brief spring shower lasting only a few minutes, with the sun quickly reappearing. They arrived at the riverbank and sat down on a large boulder to dry themselves in the early afternoon sun. Soon Vara got up to hunt for the lamb's quarters with Davide sprawled out on the smooth rock basking in the warm rays. Returned with the leaves and approaching the boulder, Vara saw a large water-moccasin, stretched out five feet long, sunning itself, with its head not far from Davide, who was blissfully watching the river flow by. Silently she crept up behind the snake and grabbed it by the tail and started swinging it around like a windmill. Davide jumped up, horrified.

Vara laughed and indicated with her free hand to her mouth, "*muy Bueno, muy Bueno. Comer.*"

Davide shook his head violently and said, "No!" The thought of eating a snake was revolting.

She then flung the snake out into the river and said in Catawban, "Go to Uktena and give Him best regards from Davide and Vara and tell

Uktena that because of Davide's mercy, Uktena should always protect him from being snake-bitten."

Of course, Davide did not understand what was said, but he heard the word Uktena mentioned several times, so he asked, "What is Uktena?"

In rough language and pantomime, she described Uktena as a part snake and part bird and part fish and part man, who lived in rivers, lakes, and caves and particularly liked to frequent the gorge beyond Table Rock, pointing in the direction of west.

Vara thought about the snake's unusual behavior, lounging next to Davide and looked at Davide and whispered in all seriousness, "The snake acted so strange, maybe he was Uktena!" but she said it in Catawban, which Davide did not yet understand.

Sergeant Hernando Moyano, to a certain degree, maintained order in the garrison with his war dog. De Soto had introduced the natives of La Florida to the war dog 26 years previously, and the terror of the man-eating dogs had turned from fact into legend. But it wasn't only the Indians of Joara who were terrified of Moyano's war dog; his Spanish comrades were equally frightened. Moyano had but to release the leash and point to a person and say "*Atacá*!" and the beast would straight away attack.

When Pardo departed for Guatarí, he left orders to Moyano not to allow women inside the barracks of the fort, and to make sure the soldiers were on their best behavior with the population of Joara. For Moyano, this was easy. Fear of falling out with Moyano and his dog kept the men in disciplined order. The ease with which this potential problem was addressed gave Sergeant Moyano the free time to pursue his personal dream. He was not from the nobility of Castile. He was not going to be a Pizarro or Cortés, but he was smart and daring, and this was the New World. He would find his treasure in the ground, from whence everything else came.

Early on Moyano had made friends with Rufín and used him to interrogate any Cacique who would listen, from Confitachequi to Joara, as to where he might find gold, silver, or gems in the earth. The Caciques were not familiar with gold or silver but did esteem copper and mica. Many Caciques said that if any people knew where gold was to be found, it would be the people of Chisca, deep in the mountains to the northwest.

However, one Orata said he did know of a certain mountain by a branch of the Catawba River two days journey from Joara, where crystals could be found and even gave Moyano instructions for finding the crystal mountain. The idea of finding this treasure kept Moyano up at night. After the second barrack was constructed and Captain Pardo had been gone for a couple of weeks, activity settled down to a form of normality. Sergeant Moyano, now technically in charge of the garrison, took this lapse of activity as a cue to pursue his personal project.

Moyano left Corporal de Carnicares in charge of the fort and journeyed with Andres Suarez, the silversmith, south for two days and arrived at the village of Yssa, on a major tributary of the Catawba River. Near there, following instructions, they found the crystal mine. With pick and mattock, they filled a leather bag with crystals, some clear quartz, some white, and some reddish and harder than any crystal they had ever seen. After a day of excavating, they set out on the return trip to Joara. Moyano resolved to keep secret the result of his escapade until he could speak directly with Captain Pardo.

When Sergeant Moyano and his Irish war dog took leave of Fort San Juan for a week of prospecting, certain things began to happen. The Spanish soldiers noticed that two of the Portuguese lads had developed an easy familiarity with two beautiful Joaran girls. At the end of one day of hard work, Davide accompanied Vara across the large field toward her house in the row of waddle structures alongside Warrior Creek. It had been unseasonably hot that day for early March, and Davide had not bathed in weeks. As they passed by the elbow-bend in the creek where women normally did their morning washing of pots and clothes, Davide eyed a deep pool, perfect for bathing. He asked Vara to wait as he stripped down to his pantaloons. Davide turned his back on Vara and entered the frigid water up to his neck. When he turned around to tell Vara how cold it was, two Spanish soldiers had appeared from behind a tree. They had been following the couple.

One of the soldiers stood on the washing rocks at the edge of the stream threatening Davide if he approached out of the bathing pool and calling him a puny Portuguese Jew. His comrade made advances toward Vara. She backed up, and the man trapped her with his arms against a tree. Ironically, it was that soldier's lucky day that his crude indiscretion was only witnessed by Juancinto, alias Juan Martín de Badajoz, instead of Vara's father, or her brother or by any other member of the community; if it had been one of them, the soldier would be a dead man.

Juancinto had followed the two Spanish soldiers, who he called "gajos," as they stalked Vara and Davide on their way to the creek.

Juancinto approached silently and hid behind the same trees the soldiers had hidden behind. As quick as a viper's tongue, Juancinto had his shaving razor unsheathed and, like a monkey, was on the back of the young man holding Vara. He pulled his hair back and with his razor broke skin, from ear to ear, causing a streaming red necklace, but astutely avoiding the veins. Vara was terrified, and her deerskin, too, was covered with blood. The other soldier, who had been threatening Davide turned toward his comrade when he heard him scream. He stood paralyzed with no intention of helping. Davide emerged from the pool and put his arm around Vara.

Juancinto whispered in the ear of the frightened soldier, "Do you want me to go any deeper?"

The lad, now crying, begged, "No."

"Very well then," Juancinto dismounted and sternly warned, "If I hear about you guys molesting any of my friends, Portuguese or Spanish or Indian, I will not stop with a scratch; you will lose your heads, and your friend here will lose his balls first. Is that clear? I want to hear both of you."

"Yes, sir."

"Yes, sir."

"And if you complain to Carnicares, Moyano, or Juan Pardo, I will tell them what you did, and it will be even worse for you. And you can tell your friends you cut yourself trying to shave your scraggly beard."

The two soldiers took off scrambling up the creek toward the barracks, too ashamed to come out from the brush onto the public field.

From that moment on, the reputation of Juan Martín de Badajoz, was established as an assassin and protector of the Portuguese.

When Moyano returned from the crystal mountain he was in a very good mood. Joara Mico, who had been waiting for him, examined Moyano's bag of crystals and approved but indicated that he knew of other places where he could find better crystals. Joara Mico had brought Erbani with him to serve as a translator. Joara Mico, through Erbani, told Sergeant Moyano that he would show him where other mines were located if he did Joara Mico a favor. Erbani explained that a few years ago, the Joarans had located three mineral salt springs at the base of the mountain up above Warrior Creek. Joara Mico had authorized the building of furnaces at these locations to distill salt crystals from the water.

This discovery soon greatly reduced the need of Joara and its dependencies on salt brought down by Chiscan salt traders. It was reported that these salt traders were now at the top of the mountain to the north and ready to come down the Salt Trail into Joran territory. Joara Mico wanted Moyano, with his men and dog, to terrorize the Chriscan into never coming back to Joara.

On hearing the word "Chisca," Moyano's ears perked up. He recalled from the historical accounts of the de Soto expedition that de Soto had heard the same rumors about Chisca and gold, and although his army was deep into Cherokee territory to the south, he sent two scouts up into Chisca land to investigate. They returned, confirming the legends, but without any gold as evidence.

Sergeant Moyano eagerly accepted Joara Mico's invitation, and the war party promptly set out. It was composed of 20 Spanish soldiers and five Joaran warriors. Moyano had been informed of Juan Martín's razor-wielding antics at the Warrior Creek washing place and had decided that Juan was the type of man he wanted by his side. Moreover, he learned that during the short time they had been in Joara, Juan Martín had become somewhat proficient in crude Catawban.

Before leaving with the war party, Juancinto gave his shaving razor to Ruy and a sharp dagger to Daniel for protection against envious and prying Spanish soldiers.

After two days on the Salt Trail, the war party laid an ambush for the Chiscan traders. The next morning a group of five traders walked into the trap. Four traders were killed outright in the ensuing melee. In confusion, one trader got away, and Sergeant Moyano saw him running down the trail. Moyano instantly ordered his war dog to attack, and the beast bounded after the fugitive.

Within seconds, the dog had caught up to the poor man and leapt up and sank his jaws into the back of the poor man's neck. Moyano was first to the scene and called his dog off. Then one of the Joaran warriors appeared and without hesitation, straddled the man on the ground and grabbed his hair-lock. The warrior took out an obsidian knife blade and with the precision of a surgeon, cut the screaming traders scalp at the hairline from front to back and on both sides. Then the Joaran, with all his might, pulled the poor man's hair-lock until it left with his scalp, exposing the bloody white of his skull. The man died before the operation was completed. The Joaran warrior loosened the dead man's hair knot and then tied the black strands of the bloody scalp to his own thigh as a trophy. Juancinto thought he had seen everything in New Granada and Paraguay, but he had never witnessed anything so grotesque. However, for the Indians in his company, the event was not noteworthy.

CHAPTER 5

THE BALL GAME

JOARA
SUMMER, 1567

It was mid-summer and along about the time that the people of Joara experience the astrological event they called "Watermelon Moon." In reflection, the summer of 1567 would be the most peaceful time of the Pardo occupation of Joara.

Earlier in the year Sergeant Moyano had taken 20 Spaniards and joined with many warriors from Joara to launch an all-out assault on Chisca. This was perhaps his personal quest to settle the question left unanswered from the time of de Soto's fruitless attempt to investigate Chisca. The question that had so unsettled de Soto 26 years previously was this: "Are the rumors true that only the Chisca know where the gold is?" De Soto sent two men to explore the Chisca, but they came back empty-handed.

Daniel and Juan Martín had been deployed with Moyano, leaving only eight Spaniards along with Ruy and Davide to make up the garrison in Joara.

With not much to do on long summer afternoons, Ruy noticed that every day before sundown, several young men would gather at a fallow field just west of the settlement. These men would play a rough game with sticks and a ball, cover themselves with dust, sweat, blood, and bruises, and then bathe in the nearby creek. Ruy asked Xequina about it, and she said it was called "The Ball Game" and that if he were interested in participating then he would have to talk to Unharca, the Conjurer, whose job it was to train and protect the team.

"Why does the team need to be protected?" he asked.

She looked at Ruy as if he were stupid with those eyes that pierced him and said, "From evil spirits cast upon the players by the opposing team's Conjurer, of course." Ruy mulled this over and determined that it was not worth further activating Xequina's mockery by exploring this topic. He decided that if he wanted to learn about the ball game, the better course of action would be to consult with Erbani, Vara's brother.

Erbani explained that the rules of the ball game were simple enough. The field of play was a field any size from 100 yards to 1000 yards long. On each end of the field was a set of goalposts about three feet wide and maybe ten feet high, with a brace across the top at about six feet from the ground. The game was always played with an equal number of men on each side— that could be ten men or could be 50 men. There was one ball in the game, and it was usually made of deerskin stuffed very tightly with squirrel hair. Each player had two sticks, usually made of hickory wood. The sticks were about two and a half feet long with a spoon-like loop at the end, laced with deerskin strips and vegetable fibers to create a net.

Once in possession of the ball, a player would run toward the opposing team's goal with the ball in his racket or discard his rackets and run with the ball in his hands or biting it with his mouth. When this player encountered opposing players, who blocked his progress or tried to throw him down, he could pass the ball with his racket or his hand to a teammate, forward or backward at any time. If the ball was dropped the opposing team could pick it up with a racket or by hand and run in the opposite direction. Once the ball crossed the threshold of the goal, either thrown or carried, a point was scored for that team.

The first team to score 12 points wins the game. Erbani then explained that some players who were large and strong specialized in guarding their own goal and roughed up opposing players as they got near the goal. Other players would be the attackers who were nimble and quick on their feet, making turns every which way to elude defenders and specialized in making quick, hard, and accurate shots on the goal. Other players who could run fast with lots of stamina, occupied more of the middle of the field where they played both defense and offense and never tired of carrying the ball or fighting for it from one end of the field to the other.

Ruy was enthusiastic about everything he heard and told Erbani that he would like to learn how to play, that it looked like good exercise. Erbani laughed and said that maybe there was something about the ball game that he did not understand.

"And what is that?" asked Ruy.

"The ball game is a serious business. We take it very seriously. It is like going on the warpath and settling a score, but without the killing. Are you ready to go on the warpath for Joara?"

"Not really. But I do need some exercise and a challenge."

"OK. Let me just explain what is at stake in an important ball game. First, every significant village or Chiefdom has a ball team. The reputation and sometimes fate of the village rests upon the performance of the team. Before every game, there is much betting, and men could win or lose everything depending on the outcome of the game. Hostile tribes and rival Chiefdoms will sometimes settle their problems with a ball game instead of going to war.

"The men are now practicing for a major ball game against the Chiefdom of Guatarí. They will play the game in a few months here in Joara just before the Green Corn Ceremony. The Micos have agreed to play two out of three games to settle an issue of importance. Two important villages to the north of here, Adini and Chara, want to transfer their allegiance away from Guatarí to Joara. I don't know why the Oratas of these two places want to do this. Maybe they don't want to be protected by the Chieftess in Guatari and pay tribute to her. Maybe they want to pay tribute to us and be protected by us because we are closer, and our warriors have a good reputation and are ruled by men. The problem is that the people in Adini and Chara live in square houses, not round houses like ours, and Adini is near the headwaters of the Yadkin River, and Chara is on the Ararat River that flows into the Yadkin.

"So, by all rights, they should pay tribute to the Chiefdom of Guatari, which controls the Yadkin River like we control the Catawba, but the people of Adini and Chara don't want to be ruled by these women. The Leaders of these villages even went to your Captain Pardo and asked permission to transfer allegiance to Joara, and he said, "no." We think because he wants to preserve the peace. We are settling this issue with the ball games. We already won the first game in Guatarí last year, and if we win the next match, then Adini and Chara will begin to pay tribute to Joara. You see how important these ball games can be? Without them, there could be war and loss of life."

"Yes, now I can see, but I still want to learn how to play and perhaps help our team in practice."

"Very well then, I will talk to Unharca, the Conjurer, as the team is under his direction. He trains the team to be strong in body and spirit and protects each player from evil curses."

"Evil curses. From whom?"

"From the Conjurer of the other team, of course. He is already working his spells on the bodies and spirits of our players. He knows them all because we have already played against Guatarí and beaten them. But we know all of their players and Unharca knows all of their weaknesses and is working on spells against every player from Guatari."

"Really? I had no idea there was so much sorcery involved. Maybe Unharca will let me play with the practice team. I can run long distances, and I'm as tough as those Spanish iron nails we brought with us. If Unharca lets me play, the Guatarí Conjurer will never have seen me before. His sorcery will not work on me, and besides, I have protection of my own."

"OK, I will talk to Unharca."

The Conjurer agreed to let Ruy practice with the team, but only if Erbani began practicing too, to make the sides equal and to serve as a translator for Ruy. Erbani agreed, and so they began to run with the team. Erbani arranged to borrow rackets from some elders to use while the two boys were making their own from hickory sticks and deerskin strips for the pouch. Xequina made two deerskin loincloths for Ruy, one for practice, and the other for a real ball game, in case Ruy got to play. She also made a pair of double strength moccasins for Ruy.

Some of Ruy's comrades at the garrison made fun of Ruy's appearance as a ballplayer. Ruy only smiled and patted the pouch that Xequina had sewn onto his belt. It contained a razor that Juancinto had given him before leaving with Sergeant Moyano. He said, "Juan Martín might be with the Sergeant, but his razor is with me." This was enough to quiet the jokers, who, as they witnessed the ballplayer's practice, began to admire Ruy.

Vara made new loincloths for her brother, and obtained red rock powder with her father's permission from his medicine box. She mixed the powder with bear oil to stain the ball game loin cloths of Erbani and Ruy a dark red color.

The boys were ready, but before Unharca would let them join the practice games he staged a series of foot races among the 30 or so players. Erbani was among the slower runners, so Unharca placed him on defense. Ruy, however, was among the faster runners, particularly at longer distances. Unharca could see that Ruy had the stamina of a long-distance trail runner, so he positioned him often in the middle of the field. Ruy reflected on all the beautiful days he ran the 12 miles between his father's villa in Covilhã and the castle in Belmonte. He only rode his horse on rainy days. Toninho and Davide never understood why, and neither did Ruy, except for the fact that he enjoyed running and it made him feel stronger.

Unharca was in the habit of setting up the ball field in different places on different terrains. Once, he set the ball field on the side of a steep hill and another time with Warrior Creek crossing at mid-field. The practice game Ruy enjoyed the most took place on an unbearably hot afternoon. It was so hot that the Conjurer set both goals in the middle of Warrior Creek, about 200 yards apart.

At first, the practices were rough, particularly for Ruy, whose unfamiliarity with the game caused most of the players to laugh and joke about him, but Ruy soon held his own against them. He observed how the best players secured the ball, protected it, ran with it, passed it, and shot it into the goal. The best player, who Ruy tried to model himself after was named Ayo. He was a young warrior from Xequina's neighborhood but not from her clan. Ruy soon learned that Ayo was the designated captain of the team. He had scored the winning goal against Guatarí the year before and was now a local hero. Ruy tried to make friends with Ayo but was scoffed at.

Ayo had also been in the warrior party that had accompanied Sergeant Moyano in this first raid against the Chisca salt traders. The young man was making a name for himself and had recently decided that the time had come to choose a wife. As tradition would have it, Ayo would begin his courtship at the upcoming Green Corn Ceremony, celebrated in the late summer, after the Ball Game with Guatarí. Ayo's eyes were set on Xequina, the neighborhood girl he had grown up with and whose warrior spirit complemented his own. Ayo had observed Xequina's friendship and affinity for Ruy and resented it to the point of obsession.

Ruy got better with each practice. And as his skills improved, it provoked some jealousy in a few teammates. During the melee of the practice games, Ruy often found himself gouged with the end of a racket or tripped-up, not only by opposing players but also by men on his own side. Ruy held his temper and worked to become more agile and shifty on the run. Unharca took notice and promoted Ruy to the first team. Ayo protested this on the basis that Ruy did not belong to any of the seven clans in Joara, and, as such, he would not have the blessing of the clans and could not represent the town.

Unharca was primarily concerned with winning. He declared that Ruy, by his ability, had earned a place on the team. Ayo challenged this and convinced Unharca to put himself on the practice team, in order to face Ruy and see if he could discourage the foreigner from playing, or at least find out what his weaknesses were. The Conjurer consented to this test, and Ayo joined the practice team. As expected, he began to target Ruy, obstructing him, whacking his legs with rackets, tripping him, and wrestling him to the ground. Ruy was up for the test, and it only improved in his ability to out-maneuver Ayo. The captain's protestations began to fall on deaf ears, and he soon gave up his campaign against Ruy and accepted his inclusion on the team. *'On the positive side,'* Ayo thought, *'if Joara loses to Guatarí, then Ruy's inclusion on the team will be the first excuse for the disaster.'*

After practice, the players normally bathed in the creek. Ruy would join them in the creek and after bathing would change into his uniform. He would then go to the house of Vara and Erbani, where there would be extra portions of meat procured by the girls while cooking at the soldier's kitchen. Unharca, the Conjurer, found out about this routine from Vara's father. He advised the girls that if they were going to do this, then they should procure only bear meat or deer, and preferable the former. They were forbidden to supplement the diet of the boys with rabbit or frog legs. When asked why these prohibitions they were informed that the rabbit was an animal easily confused and frightened, and a frog's legs were easily broken. In the afternoon Vara assembled herbs from her garden for poultices to use on the cuts and bruises the boys sustained daily.

On the morning of the great game, the team from Joara ran in a single file in a slow jog along the path beside Warrior Creek. The path passed through five neighborhoods of cheering women and children and terminated where the bold creek flowed into the Catawba River. The menfolk had departed the previous night for the ball field up-river. There, on the bank of the river, a dozen canoes were waiting for the team to paddle only a mile upstream to the great meadowlands where the ball games were normally played.

The canoes, in a single file, pulled up to the riverbank near where the playing field had been laid out and where hundreds of anxious spectators were congregating. It was here that the Ceremony of the Scratching began[2] As the players emerged from the canoes one by one, the Conjurer's assistant began the scratching ordeal. The assistant had a comb made of seven sharp splinters of turkey bone tied together on a wooden frame. The turkey, Ruy learned, was considered a war-like bird. The Conjurer's assistant scratched each player four times on the upper and lower arms and then four times on the upper and lower legs. The scratches were not deep, but were painful, and brought blood trickling down the extremities. The players next went into the river to wash off the blood. When they came out, they rubbed their bodies with slippery elm oil to make them harder to catch and hold onto.

When all the scratching, bathing, and oiling was done, the Conjurer assembled the team together and went to each player to remind them who on the opposing time was their personal enemy, and how soundly these opposing players were cursed and how favorable the omens were for that player to have a successful performance for Joara. When this was done, Unharca gathered the team together and stoked their emotions into a frenzy culminating in one long shout, in unison, proclaiming their upcoming victory as unstoppable as next spring's floodwaters.

Next, the players on both teams marched onto the field in single file. By now, there was a great crowd of spectators. Many from Guatarí had already been in the Meadowland for two or three days. Of course, there were many more spectators from Joara, including all Ruy's comrades from the garrison. After seeing the players on the field, the final bets were cast, and it was time to play.

An old man with a ball in hand walked to the middle of the field and gathered the players around him to explain the rules and caution them about good sportsmanship and fair play. He advised them not to bring weapons or potions onto the field of play and to refrain from fighting among themselves to the detriment of the game. Before the old man could finish, the Conjurer of the Guatarí team came onto the field, protesting the presence of a "bearded Spaniard" on the Joara team. The old man conferred with both Conjurers and then decided to let Ruy play.

The ball field was 500 yards long and 100 yards wide, bordered on two sides by the Catawba River. There were 15 players on each team, with five substitutes in case of injury. As the players took their places on the field, Ayo scanned the crowd for Xequina. He made eye contact and smiled. She smiled back, but then shifted her gaze to the large, bearded man with the blood-red loincloth. Ruy placed his hand over the leather medallion tied on his chest that Xequina had helped him make. Xequina had drawn the outline of a stag on the front of the medallion. On the backside of the leather piece, Ruy made the form of a Star of David to cover his beating heart. These designs were branded into the leather with Juancinto's shaving razor which had glowed with heat from the stoked embers of a fire.

The old man in the center of the field shouted, "Now for the 12!" and threw the ball up into the air.

After four hours of playing the game without rest, the Joaran side was ahead 11 goals to 10. All the players were exhausted. One Joaran defender suffered a broken leg and was substituted by Erbani. The Guatarí side, detecting an inferior player in Erbani, focused its attack on him. Guatarí scored a goal and evened the score. Erbani took the blame for the goal.

Ayo had scored four of Joara's 11 goals, and Ruy had scored one, but he had spent most of his energy running in the middle of the field from goal to goal.

Two players from Guatarí went to the sideline and obtained from their assistant Conjurer a deer bladder full of liquid. They re-entered the field of play and waited for an opportunity to intercept Ayo. Running down the field, Ayo was hit from behind by a Guatarí player barreling into him. He fell to the ground, and the two Guatarí players with the bladder emptied the bag upon Ayo's chest, soaking him with a foul liquid. The Guatarí players laughed and informed Ayo that the soup was made from rabbits with their hamstring muscles cut, then boiled alive.

Ayo also laughed, jumped up, and shouted, "That magic is nonsense." Nevertheless, the thought of the hamstrung rabbits lingered in his mind, powerfully supported by the smell of the noxious concoction mixed with his body's sweat.

Ayo was quickly back in the flow of the game. He intercepted a pass from an opposing player and began a torturous zigzag run toward the Guatarí goal about 100 yards away. Ruy ran a few yards ahead of Ayo to divert the attack and shield the ball carrier. Ruy could hear Ayo behind him, urging him on. They were 30 yards from the goal and closing in on it when, suddenly, a howl issued from Ayo's mouth. Ruy turned around and saw that Ayo had pulled up to a stop and was grasping his left hamstring muscle. With a racket in his right hand, he passed the ball to Ruy, who caught it and ran into the growing clamor of opposing rackets beating at Ruy from all sides. Ruy managed to retreat from the melee, giving himself a moment to take the leather ball from his racket and put it to his mouth, biting down on the leather with his teeth. Then, using both rackets to shield himself from blows on both sides, he again entered the battle fray, twisting and turning in the direction of the goal. Walking over fallen players and dragging others with him, Ruy was three yards away from the goal when all went black for him.

In the netting of one of the Guatarí rackets was a round stone the size of a large apple. The racket swung toward Ruy's head, and the rock made solid contact with the back of Ruy's skull. He fell to the ground, unconscious without losing the ball, still tightly held in his mouth.

Erbani arrived to aid Ruy, having run from the opposite end of the field. At the same time, Ayo picked himself up and hobbled to the scene of the fray in front of the Guatarí goal. Ayo immediately ordered his teammates to form a defensive perimeter of swinging rackets around the limp body of Ruy. Erbani grabbed Ruy's red belt and loincloth and began dragging him toward the goal. Blocking the way were two Guatarí defenders. Ayo threw his body against them, knocking them to the ground, as Erbani dragged Ruy's unconscious body across the goal line. Ruy's head entered the goal with the ball was still firmly clinched in his mouth. The game was over. Joara had won the allegiance of Adini and Chara.

As bets were settled along the sidelines, Ruy's teammates carried his still limp body over to the edge of the river. There they were met by Xequina, Vara, and Davide, and most of the members of the garrison. Ruy was carried into the river, the ball still between his teeth. Davide pried the ball out and began to sing softly in Ruy's ear songs in Hebrew and Portuguese. Still floating in the astral world, Ruy became aware of the cooling sensation of rushing water, and fingers on his body. Then he heard familiar sounds in his ears. He opened his emerald eyes to see Xequina's smile and joyous face. She exclaimed in Catawban what Ruy understood perfectly, "You are not dreaming. You won the game!"

CHAPTER 6

THE THUNDER BOYS ARRIVE

JOARA
SUMMER 1567

Regaining consciousness, Ruy was told and retold how it was that he, with the help of Ayo and Erbani, won the ball game. As the post-game festivities subsided, Xequina informed her new local hero of a pleasant surprise that she, Vara, and Davide had planned. They had arranged for two canoes to be available to them after the game. The plan for the five, now with Ruy and Erbani, was to canoe back down the Catawba past Warrior Creek for a few more miles to the juncture with the San Juan River. Then, paddle up that river three miles to the hunting cabin of Vara's father beside his cornfields. There they would rest, cook supper, and let the night play out.

Vara, her brother, and Davide took the lead in a larger canoe. Xequina and Ruy launched out into the current behind them. Xequina insisted on steering and located herself at the rear of the boat, positioning Ruy on his back with his head in her lap. Ruy rested his arms on her bare legs with his hands clasping her calloused heels, now shorn of her moccasins. Though he was battle-weary, he marveled at the perfection of her calves, long and graceful, yet strong, and smooth, without body hair. He thought, '*how is that?*' Xequina began singing softly what sounded to Ruy as a Catawban lullaby. It was still three hours before sunset, and Ruy felt the warmth of the summer sun on his face and chest. He closed his eyes and listened to Xequina's lilting voice.

> Ge'i, ge'I hwî 'lahî
> Ge'i, ge'I hwî 'lahî
> Downstream, Downstream, you must go,
> Downstream, Downstream, you must go,

Every so often, Ruy felt fresh drops of river water rained down upon him, falling from her paddle as Xequina shifted it from starboard to port, guiding the canoe around rocks and small islands in mid-stream. He thought to himself, '*starboard and port . . . how ridiculous but useful these words seemed now.*' He was slowly slipping into sleep. He felt happier than he had been since . . . Since when? Since being with Ana Sofia . . . on the island in the Mondego. He opened his eyes and looked up to the still bright blue heaven with a few passing clouds and green branches on the riverbank gliding by. '*Where am I? It doesn't matter. I am at home. I feel love.*' He closed his eyes again. He could smell of the river, mixed with the the womanly fragrance of Xequina's body. The splash and steady stroke of her paddle rocked him as if in a cradle of love. He drifted into pleasant sleep.

The sun, now an hour above the mountains in the west, cast its rays down upon the river running east. Xequina, with Ruy's sleeping head in her lap, felt that they were riding along a river of glistening crystal. She perceived the presence of the Spirit. She said to herself, '*The Long Man of this River is giving me a strange blessing in the form of this bearded man now asleep in my lap. I am at one with this stranger. How strange?*' She felt compelled to voice a formal prayer. "Long Man! This is Xequina. Listen to me. I am one who loves you. Help us sort out our love and protect us from violence and bloodshed."

She watched a blue heron fly ahead of the canoes and thought this was a good sign.

They had been on the water for nearly an hour when they approached the cabin perched on the bank of the river. In the west, the sun was touching Table Rock, but from the south, dark early evening clouds were forming. There was a faint roll thunder and far off streaks of lightning. As the canoe slid into its berth, another crack of thunder. Ruy woke up.

Xequina made a joke about the Thunder Boys coming to congratulate the winners. Ruy looked puzzled and asked, "Who are the Thunder Boys?"

Xequina responded without thinking, "They're the sons of Kanati and Selu," as she and Erbani pulled the canoes up onto the riverbank.

"And who are Kanati and Selu?" Davide countered.

"Kanati is the Lucky Hunter, and his wife, the Goddess of Corn, is Selu," Xequina stated as a matter of fact.

"And their sons are the Thunder Boys." Ruy parroted.

"That's right. Do you really want to hear more?" Xequina inquired.

"Sure. It sounds like there's a story there." Ruy declared.

Vara interrupted, "Ruy, don't get her started! Haven't you noticed yet that Xequina has a perfect memory for any word or sound she hears? She sat at the feet of all the great storytellers and can recount word for word what they said, with every gesture. If you get her started we will be here all night, and we are hungry with food to cook." Vara turned to Erbani, "Brother, you start a fire with that milkweed seed and kindling in the bin over there."

Xequina intervened, "I'll make the fire and save a little milkweed seed for my story." Looking at Erbani, "You and Ruy relax while we cook. We will eat, and when the Thunder Boys arrive I'll begin the story."

They weren't finished eating all the fish, hominy, and beans when thunder shook the cabin and lighting lit up the gloom from one bank of the river to the other.

"Now I will begin," Xequina proclaimed, as the rain began to pelt the wood-shake roof.

***

"Kanati, the Lucky Hunter, and Selu lived beside a river not unlike this one, by a singular mountain called by travelers 'Pilot Knob,' because it was always a landmark on the horizon. Kanati and Selu had a child, a little boy, and every morning Kanati would go off into the woods and bring back game at the end of the day. He would bring back whatever they desired to eat, be it a deer or a turkey or a pheasant or a rabbit. Selu would cut up the meat beside the river, washing off the blood into the water. The little boy would accompany his mother and watch her prepare the meal.

"One morning, Kanati and Selu thought they heard laughter, as if two children were talking down by the river. Their little boy was gone all day, and when he returned, his parents asked, 'Who were you playing with this morning?'

"The kid replied, "He calls himself my older brother, and he comes from out of the water. He told me that his mother was cruel to him and threw him into the river.'

59

"On hearing this, Kanati and Selu knew that the strange boy who had befriended their son had sprung from the blood that Selu had discarded at the river's edge."

Ruy then asked Xequina, "Was it the blood from the game that Lucky Hunter brought, or was it the blood from Selu's monthly cycle?"

Xequina looked at him strangely and said, "What does it matter?"

Ruy replied, "Well it matters because . . . because . . ." He could not finish his sentence as his imagination flashed back to that last night with Ana Sofia, making love at the tip of the island in the Mondego. In his mind, he saw Ana Sofia squatting in the rippling moon-lit waters, letting the current run through her and telling Ruy 'not to worry.' In Ruy's mind's eye the character of Selu began to take on the features of Ana Sofia. Ruy now feared what Xequina's story portended for him. He thought, *'Did I leave behind in Portugal a son or daughter conceived that magical night by the moonlit waters of the Mondego River?'* Thunder struck again and he came to his senses and told himself that he would refuse to let this Indian magic confuse him.

"You're right; it does not matter. Please go on with your story, Xequina."

She continued, "Every day, the little boy went to play with his 'brother' from the river, and every day Kanati and Selu tried to see the 'river-brother,' but, like a river turtle, he went back under the water just as the couple would arrive at water's edge.

"At last Lucky Hunter told his son, 'When the river-boy comes to play, get him to wrestle with you. Hold him in your arms and holler for me.'

"The boy did this and screamed for his father. Kanati and Selu ran to the riverbank, and Kanati grabbed the wild boy. He was fighting and kicking and looked to Selu and said, 'Let me go. You threw me away!'

"Holding the wild one tight in his arms, Kanati led Selu and their son back to the house. They kept the wild boy in the house until he was tame. They soon discovered that he was very intelligent and very mischievous. He was always leading his younger brother into trouble. It was not long before they discovered that the wild boy had magical powers, and they started calling him Wild Boy.

"Wild Boy noticed that every time Lucky Hunter went into the forest toward Pilot Knob, he brought back lots of game. One day Wild Boy said to his brother, 'Let's track our father and see where he gets this game.'

"It was not long after this that Kanati decided to go hunting again. He took his bow and some feathers and went off into the forest. The boys followed and saw their father go into a swamp where reeds grew, which hunters used to make arrow shafts. Just as Kanati was about to enter the swamp, the Wild Boy converted himself into a puff of bird's down. The wind blew him up, and he alighted on Kanati's shoulder."

At this point, for dramatic effect, Xequina took a piece of the milkweed tuff and blew it in the direction of Ruy, as if it were bird's down carrying the Wild Boy.

"The Wild Boy, in the form of a floating bit bird plumage, watched Lucky Hunter make arrows. When Kanati came out of the swamp, a breeze blew Wild Boy off his shoulder and over to where his little brother was hiding. Wild Boy took his proper shape and urged his brother to continue tracking their father to see where he hunted."

Xequina continued, "Keeping out of sight, the brothers followed their father up to the mountain, climbing until he came to a certain spot. Kanati dislodged a large boulder, and at once, a deer buck sprang out of the opening. Kanati shot the deer with his bow, lifted the carcass onto his back, and started home again. The boys hurried home to be there before their father arrived.

"The boys said, 'That's all father does! When he wants meat, he just rolls back that rock and kills what comes out.'

"A few days later the boys went back to the swamp and cut some reeds and made arrows. With their little bows in hand they went up to Pilot Knob to where their father kept the game. They moved the rock over the opening, and a deer came tumbling out. Just as the boys drew back on their bowstrings, another deer came bounding out, then another and another, until the boys were so thoroughly confused that they forgot what they had come for. The deer came bounding out of the mountain until there was only one left. The boys shot all their arrows at that deer but only hit the tail. And from that day to this, all the deer tails are turned upwards."

Xequina stopped to make sure Ruy and Davide were awake.

"With all their arrows shot, the boys then saw hordes of raccoons, rabbits, and other four-legged creatures come out of the hole and escape into the forest."

Ruy interrupted Xequina, "What about the bears?"

"There were no bears at that time." she curtly answered him and continued. "After the four-legged animals had all escaped, then came great flocks of game birds, first turkeys, then pigeons, and later, partridges. They were so many that they darkened the sky.

"Kanati, at home, saw the darkened sky and heard thunder on the mountain and said, 'My bad boys are into trouble. I'll go up the mountain to see what they are doing.'"

"Kanati went up to the mountain and saw the boys standing by the open entrance to the cave. All the animals and birds had gone. Lucky Hunter was furious! As punishment, he forced his sons into the cave where he kicked the covers off four great jars that stood in a corner. Immediately, swarms of fleas, gnats, lice, and bedbugs covered the boys. The vermin crawled over their skin, biting, and stinging until the boys were nearly dead. When Kanati thought the boys had been punished enough, he knocked the insects off his sons and sat them down for a lecture.

'You rascals,' he said, 'you two have never gone hungry and never had to work for your food. But now you have let all the animals out! Now when you want a deer or a turkey, you will have to go out and hunt for it. Perhaps you will not find any game and will have to return home hungry. Now go to your mother, and I try to find something for supper.'

"The boys arrived home tired and hungry asked their mother for something to eat. 'There is no meat," said the Corn Woman, 'But wait here, and I will see if I can find something for you.'

"Selu took a basket and went off toward the storehouse. The corn crib was built on stilts, well off the ground, with a ladder leading to a small opening. The boys had never been inside the crib and wondered where all the corn and beans came from. So, as soon as Selu left the house, they followed their mother to the storehouse. The Wild Boy said to his brother, 'Let's see what she does.'

"They climbed up the back of the storehouse crib and dislodged a piece of clay between the logs so that they could look in and see their mother. They saw Selu standing in the middle of the room with her basket on the floor in front of her. She leaned over the basket and rubbed her stomach just like this." Xequina rubbed her stomach. "And the basket was half full of corn. Then Selu rubbed her armpits just her stomach just like this." Xequina rubbed her armpits. "And the basket was filled to the top with beans."

"The boys looked at each other with astonishment and said, 'Our mother is a witch. This will never do! If we eat the corn and beans, we will be poisoned. We must kill our mother.'

"Corn Mother returned to the house, and soon after, the boys followed.

"'I know your thoughts,' said Selu. 'You two little fools are going to kill me.'

"'Yes," replied the boys, "because you are a witch.'

"'You're making a big mistake, boys, but I see you are too foolish to be talked out of it. Let me, at least, tell you how to survive once you've killed me.'

"'Okay, mother,' Wild Boy replied, speaking for the two of them.

"'Well,' said Corn Woman, 'after you kill me, clear a large piece of land in front of the cabin. Make it in the round form like a circle. It won't be easy to clear all the brush and ground cover, but do it, it's important. When you have finished, drag my body seven times around the circular field. Then drag my body in the four directions, crossing at the center of the circle. After you do this, then last and most important, stay awake all night. In the morning, you'll have plenty of ripe corn in the field.'

"The boys killed their mother by hitting her on the head with their war clubs. They then cut off her head and placed it on the roof of the cabin, facing west, and they said, 'Now, mother, keep a lookout for your husband coming.'

"The boys started clearing the field but soon got lazy. Instead of clearing the whole field, they cleared only seven small plots. And then they dragged Selu's headless body only on those places, and not seven times but only twice."

"And this is why," Xequina, explained to the Ruy and Davide, "that corn grows only in a few places, not all over the world, and it is only harvested twice a year."

These Portuguese young men, in some strange way, were beginning to believe the story, and why not? Before coming to La Florida, they had never seen or tasted corn or maize, the sustainer of human life in this New World.

Xequina continued with the story. "The twosome had plenty of new corn to show their father when he came home the next day with only a rabbit to eat, but Kanati was in no mood to appreciate their industry." He could not find Selu and asked, 'Where is she?"

"The boys said, 'She was a witch and we had to kill her. Her head is on top of the cabin roof."

"Kanati found his wife's head on the roof and he was, again, furious. He said, 'You idiots! You both are so stupid, stubborn, and foolish that I should kill you right now and save the world the anguish of putting up with you. But since I am your father I must spare you, but I cannot live with you. I am going to go live with the wolves. Their cubs do not kill their mothers. They are loving parents, and in battle all the wolves stand together.' Saying this, Kanati stalked off toward the forest in the direction of the village of the wolves. But before he could enter the woods, the Wild Boy changed himself again into a tuft of milkweed seed, which the wind gently carried to Kanati's shoulder.

"Kanati strolled into the town of the wolf people and into the townhouse where they were holding council.

"'What do you want with us?' the chief asked him gruffly.

"Lucky Hunter replied, 'I have two bad sons at home. I want you to go there seven days from now and challenge my boys to a ball game.'

"The wolves knew that when Kanati said, 'challenge my boys to a ball game',' he really meant 'kill them.' The wolves promised to go and 'play ball.'

"Just at that moment, the milkweed tuft on Kanati's shoulder caught a draft of air which carried it to the column of smoke from the communal fire going up through the hole in the roof of the wolves' townhouse. When the milkweed tuft came down again in the forest nearby, the Wild Boy assumed his proper shape and ran home to tell his brother what he had heard. After leaving the village of the wolf people, Kanati did not return home. He had had enough of his boys. He set out in a western direction.

"The twosome began to get ready for the coming of the wolves. Wild Boy, being a magician, was in charge. They ran around the house in a wide circle, many times, to established a trail. They left an opening in the circle in the direction from which they expected the wolves to come. The

Boys made bundles of arrows and placed them at different places outside the circle. Then they hid in the woods, awaiting the wolves. After a few days the wolves came, many of them. They went to the house through the opening in the circle the boys had made. They did not notice the trail circling the house.

"As soon as all the wolves were inside the circle, the trail changed into a high bush fence, and there was no escape for the wolves. The twosome took up their arrows and began shooting the wolves. They killed all of them except a few that escaped through the opening, and from those few that got away we have all the wolves in the world today.

"After the incident with the wolves, some strangers from far away came to the house. They had heard that the brothers had wonderful grain from which they made bread. You see, at that ancient time, only Selu and her family had known about corn."

Xequina continued, "The Boys taught the strangers what their mother had told them about the importance and rituals of the Green Corn Ceremony, how it established justice and gave people a new fire, new energy, a new start with a clear conscience every year. But they gave the strangers only seven grains of corn. They told the strangers to plant the seeds only when they stopped for the night. Then they must stay up all night and wait for the corn to grow. By morning they would have seven ears of ripe corn. The kernels from these ears were to be planted the next night in the same manner. They were to do this every night until they reached their destination, which was eight days away. If they did this, then they would have enough corn to feed all their people. The travelers started out just fine and were confident of their success, but the sun shone very hotly on the last day. The travelers were tired, and on that last night of their trip, after planting all of their kernels, the two fell asleep while guarding their planting. They awoke to nothing. No corn at all. When they reached their settlement and explained everything to their people, the people were mad, and when they told them about the Green Corn Ceremony that they were not going to have, they were even more furious."

At this point, Ruy interrupted, "Xequina, is that the same Green Corn Ceremony that is coming up in a few weeks, at the next new moon?"

"Yes, it is the same, Ruy. You will see it then, and I will explain it." Xequina hid a certain dread that came into her voice at the mention of the upcoming Green Corn Ceremony. She resumed her narrative. "The travelers, in their shame, scrounged around and found a few kernels of corn left in the bottom of a sack. They planted these precious kernels and guarded them with the utmost attention, and the corn grew. But it grew so slowly that they would only have one crop in a year, and that crop would have to be watched and tended for the first half of the year.

"When their father did not return home after the incident with the wolves, the boys were perplexed. They decided that they needed to find him. Kanati had set out toward the west, toward the Darkening Sky. The Wild Boy took a gaming wheel, a round stone wheel called a 'chunkey,' and rolled it to the west. After a while, the chunkey wheel came back, indicating that Kanati was not in the west. He then rolled the wheel to the south, and then, north, with the same result, which indicated that their father had to be in the east. The Wild Boy then rolled the chunkey toward the Sunland, and it did not come back.

"'Let's find him!' said Wild Boy, and they set out toward the east.

"After many days of travel, the twosome came upon Lucky Hunter walking along with a little dog beside him. Kanati saw them and said, 'My bad boys, why have you come here?'

"The twosome answered, 'We always accomplish what we set out to do! We are men!'

"Kanati said, 'This dog overtook me four days ago.' and the boys knew that the dog was really the chunkey wheel that they rolled out to find their father.

"Kanati suggested that since the boys had found him, they might as well travel together. They agreed and set off.

"In his mind, Kanati still wanted to rid himself and the world of these two bad boys that he had sired. Soon the three came to a swamp, and Kanati, knowing his sons' insatiable curiosity, mentioned that there was a very strange and curious being that lived in the swamp. It was very dangerous, and the boys must, by every means, stay away from it. Then Kanati proceeded onward at a faster pace. As he predicted to himself, the twosome lagged, and the Wild Boy convinced his brother to follow him into the swamp in the hunt for this dangerous being. Indeed, in the middle of the swamp, they found a gigantic panther sleeping. The two boys shot arrows into the panther's head from every direction, but the big panther hardly woke up, paying the boys no attention. The boys came out of the swamp and raced down the trail to overtake Kanati. When they caught up with him, their father asked, 'Did you find it?'

"'Yes,' replied the boys, 'but it never hurt us because we are men!'

"Lucky Hunter was surprised but said nothing. They proceeded along the trail. After a while Kanati told the boys, 'You must be very careful. We are coming into the territory of a tribe of cannibals. They are called 'The Roasters', and if they get you they will put you into a pot, boil you, and eat you.' Kanati then subtly picked up his pace and was soon out of sight.

"The boys came to a tree that had been struck by lightning. The Wild Boy told his brother to gather up splinters from the tree. Before long, they went to the town of cannibals who came running after them and caught them. The cannibals were happy with the unexpected catch of two strangers and dragged them into their townhouse tobegin preparing for their feast. The Roasters made a great fire and put a large pot on it and brought the water to a boil. Then they seized the Wild Boy and put him in the pot. Not perturbed at seeing his wild brother in the boiling water, the natural brother began to put the lightning-hit-tree-splinters into the fire to make it hotter.

"When the cannibals thought the meat inside the pot was tender enough to eat, they lifted the pot away from the fire. As soon as they did this, a blinding light filled the townhouse, and lightning bolts began to dart from one side of the chamber to the other, striking the cannibals until all were dead. The lightning went through the smoke hole in the roof, and the two boys then found themselves standing outside the townhouse as if nothing had happened. They went down the trail running and eventually caught up with their father again.

"'What! You two are here again?'

"'Oh, yes. That is because we are great men! We never give up!", replied the brothers in unison.

"'What did the cannibals do to you?' Kanati asked.

"'They brought us to their townhouse, but they could not hurt us.'

"Kanati did not reply to this. They all walked together down the trail, but soon Lucky Hunter was out of sight again.

"The twosome had been walking east and eventually came to the end of the world, the Sunland, from where the sun comes. But the night was falling when they got there so they rested. The following morning, as dawn broke the twosome went through the sunlight and climbed up the other side of the world. There sitting together they found Kanati and Selu. They were older, and Selu's hair was white like corn silk. The two brothers were received kindly by their parents and were told that they could stay for a while, but then must go and live where the sun goes down. After seven days with their parents, the twosome left and went toward the Darkening Land, where they live now. We call them the Thunder Boys as they roll in from the west and south. Our medicine men tell us that if we are in big trouble we can call on the Thunder Boys and they might step in with a helping hand."[3]

***

Xequina, musing to herself, listened to the rain pounding on the wood-shake roof and the distant rumbling. She whispered, "It sounds like someone invoked the Thunder Boys to help you today, my love." She looked over to Ruy, but he was fast asleep.

Davide, now barely awake, mumbled, "Xequina. I have news for you. Ruy and I are from the Sunland, far to the east. Think about it: either we are Angels from Heaven or, there is no end to the earth. It is round."

Xequina pretended to take offense at this, saying, "I have just told you a sacred story, and you make a joke. What an ingrate!" The only response from Davide was the beginning of a snore. She scoffed at his sleeping body and whispered, "I hope you are cold tonight," as she pulled to herself most to the blanket covering Davide and used it to cover her body, snuggled up, and spooned next to Ruy's.

She lay for a time, reflecting before falling asleep. She thought about Davide's strange, mumbled words and their implications. *'Are these Spaniards and Portuguese men really Spirits or Angels from the Sunland, the eternal world above, or are they just men like all others, living and dying, and the world really is round with no edge or end?'* She felt Ruy's arm around her, pulling her toward him, and she thought *'what does it matter; maybe both are true.'*

Chapter 7

The Green Corn Ceremony

Joara
Late Summer 1567

Ayo and Xequina grew up together in a mixed-clan neighborhood of houses, up Warrior Creek about a half-mile north of the central "square ground" with its townhouse and mound. Because they were not of the same clan it was often conjectured that, when grown, Ayo and Xequina would make a good couple, and indeed, as children, they often fantasized along those lines.

In his teenage years, Ayo was initiated and performed his vision quest. He knew he was destined for leadership, and with this knowledge he exuded self-confidence and strength. He had already participated in raiding parties against the Chisca and their Yuchi allies. He was captain of the ball team, which had just won the allegiance and tribute of Adini and Chara from Guatarí.

Ayo was on track to be War Chief someday, and probably sooner rather than later. Maybe then, with that power, he mused, he could have more than one wife. But now he had no wife, and he could not be taken seriously as a man unless he had a wife and family. Now was the time to marry. Xequina was beautiful, and she had grown up with him. She knew him. She could be difficult, exciting, and unpredictable, but he could deal with her nature, if not tame and subdue it. Their children would be strong and intelligent. She would make a good first wife. If one day they should grow apart, or his eyes and heart strayed from her, she would surely allow him to take a second or third wife. She would always be his first wife.

It must be said that Ayo noticed Xequina's attraction to the young *"nokfilaki,"*[4] named Ruy, who Unharca, the Conjurer, had allowed on the ball team. Ayo had even had the fantasy of Xequina and the *nokflaki* she fancied having sex among the ripening corn stalks, but he refused to give this fantasy credence. Ruy had helped them win over Guatarí, but he was no Catawban and never could be. Ayo thought, '*he is a Spaniard and will soon be gone. Even if Ruy were to stay in Joara after Pardo and his men leave, just as a few Spaniards stayed in Coosa after de Soto left there, Ruy would have no clan, no protection, no defense, no future.*'

Ayo resolved not to worry about Ruy and Xequina unless, that is, Xequina were to become pregnant. Ayo vowed to himself that he would not be in a marriage to Xequina and be obliged to raise an ocean-foam child. Xequina had no brother to take such a child, and he, Ayo, would certainly not raise it.

Again, Ayo reasoned, '*with the corn ripening in the fields, and the elders setting the Green Corn Ceremony to begin 14 days after the next full moon., that does not leave much time to do what needs to be done. If I am going to marry Xequina, it needs to be recognized by all at the Green Corn Ceremony.*'

To set things in motion, Ayo had his aunt talk to Xequina's maternal aunt to convey to Xequina's mother and father his intention to ask for Xequina's hand in marriage. To his consternation an immediate reply was not forthcoming. The suspense was eating at him, so, to burn off the wasted energy, he enlisted a few of his clansmen to help him build the house far up on Warrior Creek where he envisioned bringing Xequina after the wedding.

The day of Ayo's proposal, the day that Xequina had so anticipated since the age of ten had arrived. Her aunt and mother informed her of Ayo's request for marriage. '*How curious,*' Xequina thought, '*my lack of jubilation.*' Although the days of summertime frolicking in Warrior Creek were long gone, Xequina knew that Ayo's fondness for her had not diminished, but in recent years he had not pressed himself on her, perhaps out of respect for her mother and father, and perhaps out of respect for her. Now, her parents were looking to her for a decision. It should be easy, a foregone conclusion. But it wasn't. Why not? Marriage to Ayo would establish her for the rest of her life as one of the most respected and powerful women in the Chiefdom, and even if Ayo were to take future wives, what of it? She would be the first, and certainly, no other wife would be her equal.

What was it that led her to believe that the Great Spirit had something new and unimagined in store for her? And why did she dream these dreams of a bearded man in a beautiful place with beautiful children, in a world covered by an invisible bowl separating it from the world outside of disease and death? Yes, the Spaniards had come to Joara, but they had come 26 years ago and left, just as these Spaniards would leave too. Yes, without a doubt, she was sexually attracted to Ruy and felt comfortable and free and stimulated in his presence, but he also would be gone in time, and Ayo would be permanent in Joara.

Xequina reflected on how her bountiful curiosity drew her into the orbit of the *nokfilaki* people now returning to Joara after so many years. '*Grandfather had told me about the atrocities of de Soto, but that was a different time and these Spaniards did not come marauding. Vara has been drawn to the nokfilaki named Davide, who is friend and clansman of Ruy. It is interesting how Ruy and Davide insist that though they are all from the same land across the great sea, they, and a few others, are of the tribe they called Portuguese, and they are not Spaniards, do not speak from birth the tongue of the Spaniards, and in fact, have contempt for the Spaniards. Yet that does not explain why Ruy, Davide, and the other Portuguese are here. I wonder if he will explain that to me before they all leave.*

Xequina saw that, as she began to know Ruy not as a foreigner but as a real human being, she was forgetting, or at least minimizing, the clan assumptions of matrimony between Ayo and herself. *Was that wise?* Again, she thought, '*life with Ayo would be good in the traditional sense. We would have beautiful babies. He would become War Chief, and I would be one of the most respected and powerful women in Joara. This was a forgone conclusion; married and a full life unless Ayo would leave me. But even then . . .*

'*But life with Ruy, equally virile and attractive . . . And we too would have beautiful children. But where would we live? Ruy does not have a real clan, and my clan is maybe too mad at him to accept him. In which case, we would be outcasts—no support from any but the tiny Portuguese Clan, and who knows where they would be.*

'*How strong is this love, this "amor," as Ruy says?*' Xequina knew that it was strong enough to be overwhelming. Sexual attraction was always pulling her toward Ruy's presence. She yearned to be touched by him, and he seemed to be obsessed with her, but to where would this lead? She knew that if left unchecked she would become pregnant. Could she go to the medicine man or to Vara to terminate the baby? No! Then, she and Ruy and the baby would be outcasts, and she could not live with him and their baby in the garrison with all the other Spanish *nokfilaki*, that would be impossible. The right thing to do was to be honest with herself and Ruy, and put an end to their ill-starred relationship and marry Ayo at the Green Corn Ceremony.

But that would not work. How could she marry Ayo in good faith when the real man she loved was watching?

Xequina decided to pray, and since they had recently had an encounter with the Thunder Boys, she would invoke their help. She recalled the words that she had heard her uncle recite in a time of trouble.

> *May I have your attention now? Thunder, I obey you, and you love me for it.*
> *You feed upon my soul.*
> *All night long, I am filled with Your Spirit, which is life itself.*
> *No evil can come to me.*
> *May my consciousness be weightless and free, like the movements of that agile insect,*
> *the Water Spider.*
> *Well! You know I must make a choice, and I need guidance.*
> *You know me, for I am Xequina.*

The next morning Xequina woke up with the knowledge that the Spaniards would be leaving, or at least, Ruy would be moved from Joara, and therefore, Fate would make the decision for her. In the meantime, she would indulge her passion for Ruy by being as close to him as she could be without the possibility of bearing his child. If this were to drive Ruy crazy, then so be it. She speculated to herself: *'Perhaps during the night before Ruy leaves, we will consummate our love.'* If that were to result in a child, the clan would accept it. Or, she could quickly find another man, perhaps still Ayo. Hopefully, the new baby would be brown-eyed and dark like herself. The child would look Catawban, and if she played it right the fatherhood would always be her secret.

So, her course was set. She would use her strength of discipline to keep herself from crossing the line with Ruy. At the same time, she would lure him ever closer with her wily ways until the night of his inevitable departure.

Xequina knew what she had to do about Ayo so that his respect would not suffer in the face of her rejection of him. It had been over a week since his aunt talked to her aunt. She knew he would be very anxious by now and would start coming around the house looking for signs. Therefore, she and Vara made a large pot of hominy grits, and according to custom, set it out with a spoon by the path that went by her family corn crib and house. She expected Ayo to come by, see the pot of grits, and pick up the spoon to have a taste. That would be her cue to come out and protest, saying that those grits were for someone else! And that would be the customary signal that she would not marry him, and he should know not to waste his time with her, but to choose another as the target of his affection at the Green Corn Ceremony.

And so, it came to pass. When she confronted Ayo with the spoon in his hand, he was shocked. She grabbed the spoon and turned her back and walked away.

Ayo regained his composure and shouted to Xequina as she walked away, "I can't believe what you're doing! How can you be so stupid? You are in love with the *nokfilaki* who played in the ball game. He'll be gone, and you will have ruined yourself, and if you go with him you will be throwing your destiny up into the clouds. You fool! You should have let me have the corn porridge."

Xequina kept walking. In truth, she was afraid to turn and face Ayo, but with each step away from him she felt her fate was more permanently cast and her steps became more resolute.

Preparations for the Green Corn Ceremony were now in full swing. More people than ever were coming for the ceremony in Joara, and they would be carrying Joara's New Fire back to their settlements. People were traveling from the headwaters of the Catawba in Cherokee land and the wild Gorge River beyond Table Rock. They were coming from the north near the Yadkin River, coming down the San Juan River, and Warrior Creek. From the east, they came from as far as Guaquiri on the Yadkin, and from the south from Yssa, where the Catawba turns in that direction. In truth, the people were coming to this year's Green Corn Ceromonym in Joara more to see the Spaniards than for any other specific reason.

And as such, it was good that they were coming now because there were only 10 soldiers in the garrison in Joara, while far to the west up in the mountains of Cherokee territory, in Olamico, and Cauchi there were more than 145 Spaniards. These 10 soldiers left in Joara were bothersome but manageable for the natives who were providing their daily food. There was peace in Joara. They had just won a major ball game. The people from the region knew that the gathering of Clans at Joara would be the biggest event of the year, and as a bonus, they would see for themselves the Spanish armor, swords, and perhaps a demonstration of the famous firearms.

Inside Joara Mico's residence, on the mound above the square ground, the walls of the cabin were re-plastered with white clay. Down on the square ground, the walls of the War Chief's cabin were re-plastered with red clay. All the households in the central settlement were busy cleaning house and taking out old fire ashes and cleaning their cooking utensils. The large fireplace in the square ground was cleaned of its old ashes. Then ears of new corn and other vegetables, along with snakeroot and tobacco, were spread out in the firepit within the square ground.

At this time in the pre-ceremony preparations, the men were forbidden to touch women, and no one was permitted to eat any of the new corn before the Ceremony would commence.

The Ceremony began as Joara Mico called the medicine men, priests, warriors, elders, and honored men into the large square ground at the base of the Sacred Mound and announced that the fast had begun. The fast would last during the night and following day and night. Then, they would take "*pasa*," a black drink, which when consumed in large amounts induced vomiting until the whole body was purged of uncleanliness. Copious puking by the men of the Chiefdom would ensure the happiness and well-being of the people during the coming year.

After the purging, the Mico would show the contents of his medicine bundle to all the men and then return the contents to the bundle.

On the morning of the third day, the women who cooked a large quantity of food would place the food outside the square ground. The men then broke their fast and consumed the food slowly, eating it all by noon.

It was late July 1567, and the Chief Priest was in his chamber and dressed quietly in his white buckskin, from his moccasins to the waistcoat, shoulder cape, and headdress. He then sat on the ground, straddling a flat piece of oak wood with a small hole bored in the wood. Around the hole, he gathered a handful of dry milkweed tufts, and into the hole, he inserted an oak stick, fitting tight enough in the hole to cause friction when rotated. He uttered a prayer for the new fire and the new year. Then the Chief Priest began to rotate the stick in his hands over the hole and mound of milkweed tufts. As soon as smoke appeared, he fanned the tufts with white bird feathers until the flame ignited. Next, he quickly laid splinters of pinewood soaked in sap upon the little mound.

Within a few minutes, the New Fire was established. The Chief Priest put the fire in a clay vessel, and carried it to the center of the large fire pit in the middle of the square ground. Baskets of fruit and vegetables were then brought to the priest. He selected some, and then rubbed the food with bear oil and placed it in the fire. The foods caught fire and were supplemented with more food and wood until an enormous bonfire blazed.

The priest instructed all the women in the town to go to their houses and extinguish their fires, on penalty of being impure and bringing divine punishment upon the town. The women scurried off to their homes. During the next hour, in the surrounding hills cradling Joara, last year's cooking fires were extinguished.

Into the afternoon sky, smoke billowed from the New Fire in the center of the square ground. In contrast, on the north side of the mound and square ground, where the Spanish complex was located, four small columns of smoke rose from fires that continued to burn from the previous year. This was not a good omen.

The Chief Priest gazed over at the smoke from the Spanish plaza as he began to lecture the people of Joara on the necessity for obedience to the town customs and rules. He cautioned about not breaking the rules regarding marriage and sexual propriety. He warned about gossip and going crazy from jealousy. He asserted that if Joara failed to abide by the rules and established customs, they could expect drought or floods at the hands of the Thunder Boys, disease by witchcraft, and slavery and death at the hands of their enemies.

Meanwhile, six older women began to dance, carrying bundles of tree branches. They were joined by the other priests carrying similar bundles to build the fire. They stomped their feet with short quick steps and sang sacred songs to the drumbeat.

The women of Joara carried new fires back to their houses. When they returned to the square ground the great feast began. There was dried meat, fish, corn, beans, pumpkin, squash, and wild fruit for everyone.

Night fell. The musicians carried the beat and song with gourd rattles and drums made of pottery and deerskin. The dancing never stopped. Near the end of the festivities, the men began to decorate themselves with war paint and took up their weapons in a mock battle. Ayo was among the warriors leading the dance. As they danced, the warriors asked their chosen women to join them. Perhaps to offer Xequina one last chance to change her mind, or perhaps to publicly humiliate her, Ayo signaled to Xequina to join him in the dance. She refused, and as a result, the Chief Priest publicly shamed her and imposed upon her family a fine. She was indignant toward the Chief Priest and shouted at Ayo as she stormed off into the night.

The dancing lasted till dawn when the Chief Priest announced that the Green Corn Ceremony was over. The town was pure again with a fresh start in the coming year. To symbolize this, the Chief Priest painted himself with white clay. Then all the people followed the Chief Priest in a single file according to their importance in the social order. They first marched to the pit with the white clay mud and coated themselves with the substance, then they proceeded to the bathing pool by the washing area of Warrior Creek. There, following the priest, they immersed themselves in the water, washing off the clay. Next, they returned to their homes, villages, and settlements to start the new year.

Xequina observed this ritual washing from behind a group of large boulders overlooking the bathing pool. Her fury at being singled out by Ayo and the Chief Priest slowly subsided. In its place was a sense of sadness at the realization that the Great Spirit was separating her from her people. The reason was not yet clear. She wondered, '*will I ever be cleansed again and made pure by the waters of Warrior Creek?*'

CHAPTER 8

SEARCHING FOR LA GRAN COPALA

CHISCA TOWN- SPRING 1567
OLAMICO ISLAND- SUMMER 1567
THE BIG SUCK- AUTUMN 1567

Earlier in the year, when Sergeant Moyano returned from his ambush of the Chiscan salt traders, he wrote a letter to Captain Pardo describing the event and asking permission to go further into the interior using military aggression when necessary. He sent this letter back to Santa Elena by way of a Spanish runner. No sooner had he dispatched the runner when an Indian messenger came down the trail from the north carrying a message from a mountain Cacique, probably from Chisca. The message was that the Cacique was "going to kill and eat all the Spaniards, including the dog."

Moyano took this personally. He did not wait for Juan Pardo's reply but organized another war party composed of 20 of the remaining 30 Spanish soldiers at Fort San Juan and many more Joaran warriors. Daniel and Juancinto were part of this war party.

The soldiers journeyed for the better part of a week up through and over the mountains and eventually followed the Nolichucky River in a westerly direction. When they reached the main Chisca town they saw it was heavily fortified by high wooden palisades and only had a small wooden door. The chiscan warriors had anticipated the arrival of the Spanish. As Moyano's party approached a shower of arrows rained upon them from atop the palisade wall. Using their shields to protect them from them from the arrows, Moyano, after sustaining a wound in the mouth, finally gained entry through the small door.

As the Spaniards entered the structure, the Chiscans retreated to their earth-covered homes, using them as cover in the skirmish with the

Spaniards. The Chiscans were now barricaded in homes which would not support a flame. The Spaniards then set fires in the small doorways and plugged up the chimney holes. Those that tried to escape the smoke-filled chambers were shot with arrows and crossbow lead. Moyano declared that he and his men had killed 1,500 natives, although many disputed this as an exaggeration.

To the Chiscan culture it was annihilation, and to the warriors of Joara who had never participated in this degree of devastation it was sobering. Their concept of war had been centered around ambush, hit and run, with harassment and looting, more of a sport than genocide. Only the wise elders had remembered the stories of the extermination that occurred when de Soto rampaged through the country.

It was the middle of May 1567 when Moyano, still camped at the ruins of the Chisca town and searching for gold and mines in the surrounding mountains, received Captain Pardo's reply to his letter sent two and a half months before. In short, Juan Pardo encouraged Sergeant Moyano to continue his exploration into the interior. This was the signal Moyano had been waiting for. He took his 20 men and a few Indian guides and proceeded along the Nolichucky west to where it flowed into a larger river, which came to be called the French Broad River.

***

It is noteworthy to observe that, in all probability, very few Joaran warriors elected to follow or, perhaps, were permitted to follow, and join Sergeant Moyano's group as it continued in the mountains. Joara's economic trade rival, Chisca, had been eliminated, and now Joara had all the salt trade in the Catawba and Yadkin Valleys. Toward this end Joara had been victorious, but at the cost of witnessing the utter destruction of their competitive rival. Perhaps the same victory could have been achieved with a simple ball game.

***

After traveling two more days along the French Broad River, Moyano's party reached the Chiefdom of Chiaha. They were now in Creek territory under the authority of the powerful Mico of Coosa, located many leagues to the south. Paddling down the river in a file of canoes, they came to a great island with a width of one-third of a mile and a length of two and a half miles. The island was called Olamico and was one of the centers of the Chiaha Chiefdom. Olamico's defense was a strong palisade with square towers, and in the center was a ceremonial mound, 30 feet high.

When Moyano and his men arrived at Olamico, they found no women and children present, only warriors, as if they were anticipating an attack like the one waged by de Soto 26 years previous. Judging by the number of warriors congregated in Olamico, Moyano was apprehensive and rather than attack sought peace like Captain Pardo had done in Joara. But unlike in Joara, where after adjusting to the presence of the Spaniards, a semblance of ordinary village life went on, in Olamico most of the women and children were withdrawn from the island.

The Orata of Chiaha together with the Orata of Olamico and their entourage of warriors and women food-preparers visited the island daily and interacted with Moyano and his men, but the atmosphere was not natural considering the myriad of cook fires coming from the hills on each side of the river. Olamico, this big island with palisades and Sacred Mound and a ceremonial center, became Moyano's headquarters for the time being. Near the mound, just as in Joara, Moyano had his men built a small fort while he awaited Captain Pardo's arrival.

Over the summer months of 1567, while in the rolling hills of Joara, Ruy was participating in the famous ball game and Xequina was turning her back on Ayo at the Green Corn Ceremony, across the Blue Ridge, Moyano and his 20 men maintained a strange peace on the river island while living off the largess of a population that barely showed itself, but for a few, mostly women, who supplied them with subsistence rations. As Moyano wrote to Captain Pardo, they were "surrounded by Indians" that were not friendly but were not at war— a strange peace or accommodation maintained without violence. To Moyano the boredom was intolerable. The Orata of Olamico, perceiving that Sergeant Moyano was a man ruled by greed for objects from the earth, lured him off the island accompanied by a prospecting party of his soldiers. They spent weeks marching up and down the surrounding mountains following up false leads supplied by the Orata and his headman, always returning to the island empty-handed and waiting for Captain Pardo to liberate them from this strangeness.

Earlier the news of the massacre at Chisca had reached Olamico by runner, in less than 24-hours after the tragic event. Then south by river and trail, the news traveled to Coosa, under which Olamico and Chiaha had pledged loyalty. Within four days of the massacre at Chisca the Chiefdom of Coosa began to prepare for a recurrence of the "days of de Soto." The memory of those trajic days was still alive and fresh after 26 years. De Soto had devastated the large town of Coosa and taken much of its population, including royalty, as slaves to be used or bartered.

Those Coosa warriors who escaped the calamity of the days of de Soto banded with other Creek and Cherokee warriors. They went further south to fight under the leadership of the great Creek Chief Tuscaloosa. Thousands of these warriors under Tuscaloosa encountered the army of de Soto at a place called Mabilia. For every Spaniard who died, at least ten, to perhaps 100 warriors died, but it was not a victory for the Spaniards because most of their horses were shot out from underneath them.

The Spaniards never recovered from the blow. They managed to make it to the great river, called 'Mississippi,' but not without the loss of many men to constant skirmishes, coupled with fatigue, sickness, lack of food, and internal dissension. Hernando de Soto either died of illness or was killed on the banks of the Mississippi River, and a remnant of his men made it down the great river to the Gulf and eventually to Spanish territory to tell the story.

To the Cherokee and Creek, the confrontation with de Soto did not end in defeat but with an eventual victory. After all, the Spaniards had kept away and stayed out of their lives for 26 years. But now they were back, and the memory of how to defeat the Spanish enemy had survived in the minds of the Indian leaders.

When the news of the Chisca massacre had reached Coosa Mico, this Chief had already been informed of Juan Pardo's building of Fort San Juan in Joara and Pardo's return to his home base in Santa Elena. He expected Juan Pardo to return to Joara and the mountains beyond with a large army. Indeed, this is what Sergeant Moyano, in charge of the Spanish detachment, made no secret to continually affirm to his men and those that provided them hospitality. Therefore, this is what Coosa Mico, Chiaha Orata, Olamico Orata and the dozen or so other Chiefdoms of the various river valleys were expecting.

To exterminate Moyano and his 20 men now in Olamico would be child's play, even though they may lose 200 warriors in the act, and this action would only alert the Spaniards for a major battle and cause them to prepare for it. Much better to keep Moyano and his men as bait or hostage on friendly terms, until all the Spanish army, under Pardo and Moyano, could be ambushed and killed at once.

Daniel and Juancinto participated in two of Moyano's initial forways into the surrounding mountain recesses looking for gold and gems. But they soon understood that their Sergeant was being manipulated by his obsessive passions, and they were sick of marching up mountains and pointless digging. They prevailed upon the Morano to let them stay with those who were manning the small fort and concentrate on learning the Creek language and possibly learn why the menfolk were absent.

By now both Daniel and Juancinto had come to the realization that their fate and destiny would be determined in this wild land. There would be no return to Europe. Here their lives would be played out. For Juancinto, this was but the culmination of a life of adventure, and he would adapt accordingly, but for the young Daniel, this was a land of infinite possibilities, and he was up for the task of achieving greatness in the New World.

Since his days in Paraguay with Nani at the leper colony, Juancinto had come to regard his guitar as his most useful possession, even surpassing his razor and his sword. With his music he could bring joy to the depressed and calm the agitated; he could heal and cause to dance. Nani had even taught him how to use his guitar to pray.

Juancinto, with time on his hands, now used his guitar to turn the horror of what he had witnessed at Chisca into a mournful melody. While practicing near the open kitchen, he noticed some women preparing food moving to his music. He stepped up the beat, which was amplified by a passing young man with a hand drum. Among the women dancing was Immokalee, the daughter of the Olamico Orata.

To cultivate this new-found audience, Juancinto began playing every day by the open kitchen while the women cooked, and he soon became familiar with the inquisitive Immokalee. Juancinto sang for her a *palos gitanos*[5] ballad in Castellano, followed by a short song in Muisca that he created as a tribute to Atora, and another in Guarani that Nani had taught him.

Intrigued by Juancinto's embrace of music and language, Immokalee tried to ask Juancinto to put into music the words of prayer she liked to recite. Juancinto looked into her eyes, and then he looked away for fear of being sucked into her presence and losing his balance. Putting a safe distance between Immokalee's heart and his own, he saw in her a youthful figure, an image that subtly morphed between his memories of Solea, Atora, and Nani.

Juancinto returned to his senses and indicated that he did not understand what Immokalee was asking because he had not learned the Creek language. When this was deciphered, with the help of the surrounding women, Immokalee made it clear that Juancinto did not have to understand her words, just give her music to which she could dance so-as-to put her prayer in motion.

When this was understood, Juancinto found this challenge irresistible, but to protect himself personally from the strange allure of Immokalee, he suggested, "I have a friend who is here. His name is Daniel. You might have seen him. He is about your age. He and I are trying to learn to speak Creek, and we need a teacher. I will put your prayer to music if you help us to speak your language."

With no hesitation, Immokalee agreed. She was a free spirit with headstrong determination, accustomed to finding a way to get what she wanted.

Daniel and Juancinto set out to learn the Creek language with Immokalee using the same techniques that Rufín had taught them back at Santa Elena, the same methods they all had used at Joara. True to Juancinto's promise, they used Immokalee's prayer for their frame of reference. Eventually, they rendered the prayer into Spanish and Portuguese.

IMMOKALEE'S PRAYER

Ku! In your High Heaven YOU repose.
Ku! Oh, Great and Terrifying Woman, wake-up!
YOU have drawn near to hear.
In your High Heaven, YOU are at rest, Oh White Woman,
No one is ever lonely with YOU,

YOU are Most Beautiful.
Instantly and, at once, YOU have rendered me a white woman.
No one will ever be lonely with me.
YOU have made the path white for me.
It shall never be dreary.
Now YOU have put me into it.
YOU have brought down to me from Above, the white path.
Here on the surface of the earth,
YOU have placed me.
I shall stand erect on the earth.
No one will ever be lonely with me.
I am beautiful.
Peace and security radiate around me.
No one will ever be lonely with me.
When my man comes who YOU have allotted for me,
let him put his soul at the very center of my soul,
never to turn away,
even in-the-midst of other women.
I shall never become blue.
I am covered by an everlasting white house, wherever I go.
No one is ever lonely with me.[6]

Daniel was perplexed and asked why she wanted to be white and pointed to his skin. Immoka laughed and indicated that his skin was not white. Juancinto, intrigued, asked her what was so good about the color white. Befuddled, she tried to explain that "white" stood for peace and happiness in all their stories, prayers and sacred formulas. "It can mean something clean and fresh, like in our Green-Corn dance, the speaker invites the people to come along the white path and enter the white house and partake of the new white food."[7]

Little by little, word by word, Daniel and Juancinto translated the prayer and were astonished at its strangeness, audacity, and frankness. By the same measure, Immokalee learned to say the prayer in Spanish, and when this was accomplished, she said, "It is not enough. I want to sing it and dance it!"

Daniel and Juancinto conferred and debated about what European style of music could possibly capture the intent of the prayer in song and dance. They finally settled on a troubadour style of love poems with Arabic rhythms that Daniel had heard performed in Fez and at the Camel Bazaar outside Ceuta. It had a fateful sound like the *fados* of Coimbra, but not as heavy and mournful, and with a North African beat and rhythm that was danceable and not unlike what was natural to the Indians of those mountains. Juancinto could not resist embellishing the distance between stanzas with a "*palos gitanos*" chorus based around the words "no one is ever lonely with me."

After Immokalee quickly learned to sing the prayer in Spanish, for good measure, she had Juancinto privately teach her to sing it in his version of Portuguese. This was to be a surprise for Daniel to be displayed when the time was right.

Juancinto saw it coming from the beginning, perhaps as a premonition, even before the day that Daniel met Immokalee. On that day Daniel was immediately enchanted by her presence. And, to his credit, Daniel comported himself naturally with the qualities that Immokalee saw in a Great Warrior.

As the long summer days passed with studying Creek and Spanish, Immokalee became ever inwardly convinced that she was destined to sing and dance her prayer only for Daniel. But, of course, she kept this to herself and coyly dodged his advances. When she finally performed her dance and prayer in Portuguese, privately for him by the light of a full moon and campfire, he was hopelessly drawn to her, like a moth to flame.

Juancinto and Daniel, for their part, learned to speak and understand rudimentary Creek. After progress in Catawban and Cherokee, it was easier.

During their lessons, Immokalee often brought up the stories of how de Soto and his army stayed at Olamico before going south. She said that the storytellers related that de Soto was always looking for a way to a special place that he had heard about. He called it "La Gran Copala," and it was a city of tall stone houses filled with pearls, gold, and silver. Immokalee had heard of this legend also and believed in it. She had heard from storytellers that this fabulous city was only eight days away traveling various rivers west and south of Olamico.

This story first played on Daniel's fancy and imagination and slowly succeeded in dominating his thoughts. '*La Gran Copala is the El Dorado that de Soto was always looking for. Immokalee says it is only eight days away by river. We are so close. With her as guide and interpreter, and with Juancinto for good measure, we could get there and return in a month. We could accomplish what de Soto and countless others gave up their lives for. We would be rich and famous. Perhaps this is the purpose of our strange odyssey!'*

Daniel commenced to seriously question Immokalee as to her experience on the rivers to the west. She said she had been as far as two days down the French Broad to where it meets with the river Holston. "It is within Cherokee land, and there is a trading post there." Beyond that, she did not know, but she was a good paddler and could navigate through and around rapids. She was willing to accompany Daniel to find La Gran Copala, wherever it was.

Next, Daniel broached his plan to Juancinto. On fully understanding that the quest that Daniel was proposing for La Gran Copala was the same as de Soto's hunt for El Dorado, Juancinto had nothing but scoffing contempt for the whole idea. Juancinto explained to Daniel the real meaning and origin of the term, El Dorado, a knowledge he had gained first-hand in Muisca land and said he wanted nothing to do with the fool's errand.

Daniel was profoundly affected by Juancinto's story and began to appreciate him even more as a man of many facets and deep levels of life experience. Nevertheless, Daniel was determined to proceed on his plan with Immokalee. When Juancinto realized that he could not reason Daniel out of the fantasy of La Gran Copala, he began to look at this inevitable escapade from another angle.

"Daniel," he ventured, "you'll need a good canoe and plenty of provisions, along with a crossbow with plenty of lead, your sword, and armor, among other things. Immokalee wants to go with you, God knows why but she does. The atmosphere here in our little fort on Olamico Island is heavy and strange. Any day now we may be attacked by a thousand Indians, or Captain Pardo may show up. If you go searching now for La Gran Copala and don't find it, you cannot come back. You will be regarded as a deserter, and God knows what will happen to Immokalee. But if we go to Sergeant Moyano and explain to him our plan to find La Gran Copala eight days away by way of the rivers, with

Immokalee, we can tell him that if we do find the Treasured City, we will return to Olamico and not only report to him but to lead him to it."

Juancinto continued, "We will explain to Moyano that Immokalee will not tell her father she is going with us. Therefore, when Olamico Orata finds out we are gone, he will regard Immokalee as our hostage and may not attack us or stop an attack under which we are so outnumbered for fear of losing his daughter. If the Sergeant agrees, then he will provide us with the things we need for the trip. and in that case, yes, I will be going with you. The Sergeant must get for us with two good canoes and all the provisions and weapons we need. If we fail, then, at least, we can come back."

Daniel could see the perfect reason for this plan, and together with Juancinto sought out Sergeant Moyano to get his blessing. The idea appealed to the Sergeant's avarice for wealth and the idea of the Orata's daughter as a hostage soothed his apprehension of an impending attack. He granted permission, and by the next morning, the three were on their way to find La Gran Copala.

Immokalee proved to be a natural adventurist with a brave heart. She placed herself in the bow of the lead poplar trunk-canoe with Daniel in the stern and Juancinto following in the second canoe. Immokalee guided them around dangerous rapids and hazardous rocks hiding beneath the surface of the fast-moving river.

By nightfall, they had already reached the trading post at the convergence of the French Broad and Holston rivers. After this junction, the river became known as the Tanasqui, or what came to be called the Tennessee River. From here, for the next six days, the journey was ideal with few rapids, a good current, and beautiful scenery through the drainage of a large valley. After the sixth day, they reached the juncture with the Hiwassee River.

By now, the river in some places was a half-mile wide. Late in the afternoon of the seventh day, looming before them they saw a range of green mountains seemingly blocking the path of the river. The wide river began to narrow and follow its circuitous route around and through the mountain impasse. All had gone well so far, and expectations were running high. By the nightfall of that day, the travelers had reached the cooking fires of the town of the Napochies on the left bank of the deep river.

The Napochies were a tribe that was under the alliance dominated by Coosa. A few years in the past, they had staged an unsuccessful rebellion against Coosa and now were obliged to pay a special tribute to that paramount Chiefdom. Daniel and Juancinto did not display any of the weaponry or accouterments of European civilization, and Immokalee explained that the bearded ones in her party were second-generation descendants from de Soto's march through Olamico, and they were part of her tribe.

The Orata of Napochies told Immokalee two critical things. First, the Mico of Coosa was collaborating with all the Oratas from the towns between Coosa and Olamico and assembling thousands of warriors with the goal of exterminating the current Spanish invasion with a surprise attack. The second important piece of information was that the great city of Copala was nearby, only a day or so down the swift and turbulent river. If they could only get through a few more dangerous rapids, including the place they named Un'tiguhi, or the pot-in-the-water, they would be there. The travelers asked about the pot-in-the-water and were told that it was a place where the water boiled like that in a pot. It can become a large whirlpool in the middle of the river, and it was adjacent to a mountain creek flowing down from the right called Suck Creek. In times past, many a river traveler has been sucked into the vortex of Un'tiguhi, never to be seen again.

Duly warned, they set out the next morning under cloudy skies, and by noon they had reached a place in the river that fit the description of Un'tiguhi. They saw the waters boiling in the middle of the river and decided to pull up at the bank to develop a strategy for safely getting around the turbulence. Daniel, leaving Immokalee's canoe, climbed into Juancinto's canoe to unpack some rations for lunch.

All morning long they heard thunder among the mountains, and now the bottom of the dark clouds gave way, producing a deluge. In the pouring rain, they could see a few hundred feet ahead that Suck Creek had been transformed into a waterfall pouring into the river. Amazed at this sight, they had not noticed that boiling pot had turned into a whirlpool of concentric waves that had now reached the riverbank upon which the canoes were resting.

Then it hit. A large wave caused Immokalee's canoe to pound against Juancinto's. In an instant, Daniel jumped back into Immokalee's canoe, which was now being pulled away from the riverbank into the maelstrom. Paddling was futile as the canoe began to spin, first in a broad circle, then narrowing and picking up speed as it aimed toward the center of the spiral. Their only hope was the rope that Daniel tied securely to the canoe. The other end was left on Juancinto's canoe. Juancinto quickly took the rope tied it around a stout tree trunk on the riverbank. By now, Immokalee's canoe had reached the center of the vortex and was spinning around hopelessly. Daniel, in the stern, was practically underwater. The rope was stretched out over 30 yards and became taunt with the force of the whirlpool pulling on it.

The result was that the canoe capsized, throwing Daniel into the disappearing spiral of Un'tiguhi. Immokalee held on to the canoe as she watched Daniel's black hair and beard vanish in the foaming vortex. Juancinto struggled to reel in the capsized canoe, now lighter. The roar coming from Suck Creek seemed to quiet, and the ferocity of the whirlpool, now claiming its victim, had begun to subside.

The sun was breaking through the clouds by the time Immokalee and the capsized canoe were moored against Juancinto's canoe. Juancinto helped Immokalee into his canoe, and there they sat, his heart again broken in pieces, but not to the extent hers was. With his arms around her he tried to comfort her anguished wailing.

After half an hour of unrelenting sobbing, they began to collect themselves and take stock of their situation. There would be no more search for La Gran Copala. Their way back to Olamico would be by land following the swift rivers they had come down. Immokalee would carry the food, and Juancinto, his crossbow, sword, and guitar.

Before leaving, they decided to pull the canoes up onto the bank to be useful to whomsoever would venture by. Struggling to pull the heavy canoes up onto the riverbank, Immokalee looked down the river and saw something move and splash on the opposite bank some 60 yards away.

***

Daniel had felt himself being pulled down, as if by his ankles, with his body spinning around like a top. First foam, then swirling water.

There was so much going on that he forgot to be afraid. At a certain point, the spinning ceased, and he saw a diffused light below. He let his body sink toward a light, and as he sank closer he had begun to swim toward the light. He found himself perched on a mountain overlooking a prosperous valley of cornfields and orchards with many canals leading to a busy city dotted with many mounds topped with white buildings. Below were other buildings decorated with all the colors of the rainbow. He swam closer to see the faces of the people who seemed to be celebrating something. He did not recognize any of the faces, however, they were welcoming him, waving, and urging him to come down and take part in their festivities. He was about to do this when he felt something land on his shoulder. It was a thick rope, like the ones used on the "*Rainha de Alcântara.*"

He held onto the rope, and it pulled him away from the glorious city in a centrifugal fashion, spinning now out of the valley and above the mountains. He was thrown up onto a sandy bank of the river on the opposite side where Immokalee and Juancinto were wrestling with the canoes. His lungs convulsed, trying to expel the river water he had swallowed. Splashing and coughing he became aware of his return to the physical world. Then he heard Immohalee joyfully shouting his name.

Immokalee and Juancinto had quickly righted the capsized canoe, and using two paddles, furiously paddled upstream as they clung to the west bank until they were 300 yards above the Un'tiguhi. From there, they headed downstream, steering toward the east bank while clinging to its shore, then past the whirlpool, which was now diminished, until they reached Daniel, still trying to clear his lungs of water.

They pulled Daniel up onto the graveled-sand beach, and Immokalee smothered his body with kisses, thanking him for risking his own life to save hers. "Your soul has come back to my soul," she announced. "They are together, and we shall never be blue."

It took three weeks for the three to walk back to Olamico. Immokalee's father staged a celebration with those remaining in the village. The villagers asked if they had found La Gran Copala. Daniel could only answer, honestly, that he had found the Great City, but it was not of this world, and he could not get back there. When questioned more closely by Sergeant Moyano, he encountered skepticism and even ridicule, but Moyano did have to admit that the warriors surrounding Olamico had not attacked the fort, and perhaps it was because Immokalee was regarded as a hostage.

Within a week of their return from the adventure, Captain Juan Pardo arrived with 125 soldiers. Daniel and Juancinto were glad to see again their old friend, Guillermo Rufín, who was still accompanying Juan Pardo as his official Interpreter. The three arranged to stay together in a house nearby the tiny fort, which was now in the process of being enlarged. There was much catching up to do. Rufín reported on all the political happenings at Santa Elena while Juancinto and Daniel told about the massacre at Chisca and their recent adventure downriver looking for La Gran Copala.

CHAPTER 9

OVER THE MOUNTAINS TOWARDS

AUTUM-1567-68

Captain Juan Pardo, was now commanding his second expedition into the interior, leaving Santa Elena on September 1, 1567 with 125 men. He followed his original route directly to Joara and on September 24, entered the Chiefdom a month and a half after the Green Corn Ceremony had taken place. Arriving at Fort San Juan, Juan Pardo learned about Moyano's uneasy circumstanced at Olamico. Fearing that Sergeant Moyano and his 20 men were in imminent danger, the Captain stayed only two days in Joara.

He left the garrison at Fort San Juan staffed with the same 11 men as before, which included Ruy Gonçalves and Davide Oliviera de Mendes, much to their satisfaction, as they had adapted to and were even enjoying their new life at Joara. Juan Pardo proceeded with his expedition of 125 men, heading due west from Joara, and following the Swannanoa River as it flows down from the mountain highlands at the Black Mountain Gap.

It took two days from Joara to pass over the eastern ridge and reach the Cherokee settlement of Tocae on the bank of the French Broad River. They stayed only a few hours in Tocae before marching west along the riverbank to the crucial Indian town of Cauchi, where they met many Caciques from the area. The French Broad river, in Cauchi, was confined by a gorge. Leaving Cauchi, the soldiers walked for three days northwest following the flow of the river as it widened and descended through the mountains and hills until it reached a fertile valley.

The Spaniards compared this terrain to the best lands of Andalusia. Eventually, they came to a fortified Indian town called Tanasqui, where the French Broad River met the Nolichucky. The following day, continuing along the French Broad, they entered the territory of Chiefdom of Chiaha, and next the central island town of Olamico, bound by the river on two sides. The expedition forded the waist-high river and walked around the palisade wall of Olamico until they found the gate. They entered Olamico with no resistance from the warriors who were populating the island without many women and children.

Sergeant Moyano and his men were overjoyed to see Juan Pardo and happily guided the soldiers to Moyano's small fort by the 30-foot-high ceremonial mound. Moyano explained that they did not feel themselves in immediate danger, but they were afraid to leave the proximity of the fort and the safety of the walls surrounding the island. The warriors had been providing them with only enough food to survive. Moyano said he believed that the Indians knew that Pardo was coming. Indian message runners were always coming and going from Olamico. There was an atmosphere of waiting and expectancy. Moyano did not know what the Indians were waiting for, but his suspicions kept his men near the fort, rather than prospecting the surrounding mountains as he would prefer.

Captain Pardo met with the Orata of Olamico and the Orata of the larger Chiefdom of Chiaha at the small Spanish fort constructed at the base of the ceremonial mound. Conversing through Guillermo Rufín, always at Juan Pardo's side, the Captain bestowed gifts of axe heads, picks, and knives to the Caciques and explained that he intended to continue his march south to Coosa and then farther south to the land of the Chichimecas. The Caciques both acknowledged that Coosa was one week, perhaps two, down the trail, but they did not know of any area called Chichimeca beyond Coosa. Juan Pardo was a little perplexed at this but blamed the ignorance on bad translation. Pardo asked the Caciques for permission to ascend the mound to the council house and present a message from King Phillip of Spain to those gathered below. The Caciques consented and accompanied Juan Pardo and Rufín up the steps to the top of the mound. On reaching the top and gazing around, Juan Pardo had the same feeling he had had that first hour in Joara from atop the mound there. He saw meadowlands with cornfields over most of the island with grapevines and persimmons trees. Looking into the early October sunset, he could see through the orange gloaming the far southwestern point of the island where the river re-joined itself. There were mountainous hills and fertile valleys all around the island with cookfires from a dozen villages. The mild autumn breeze carrying the smell of fall and the wood smoke was pleasant and perfect. Juan Pardo thought to himself, *'this is truly a land of angels,'* and he was glad to be bringing the message of Salvation to these people.

Juan Pardo proceeded to give a speech to the assembled warriors of Olamico and Chiaha, the same speech that he had delivered over 30 times during the past year. Through Rufín, Captain Pardo announced that all were now subjects of the King of Spain and the Pope. The Pope and his Church taught the message of Salvation brought to all by Jesus Christ, the son of God, who gave his life to save humanity. If the Caciques requested, he would send to Chiaha monks to teach the catechism to the people. He told them that in the meantime they were expected to build a storehouse for corn and keep it filled. The ears of corn would only be used to feed the Spanish soldiers. Permission would have to be obtained from the King of Spain to break this rule.

Rufín was instructed to ask the assembled chiefs, headmen, and warriors if they agreed with all that he said. Juan Pardo expected to hear the usual "Yaa" from the crowd, but there was silence. Rufín was told to ask again, but again there was silence. Juan Pardo attributed this to a poor translation.

Captain Pardo descended the mound and walked with the Orata of Olamico from the mound to the small fort 30 yards away. Pardo's men were in the process of filling the fort with supplies they had carried on their backs. Among the items that had been transported up the mountain where many fiber sandals and leather shoes that Juan Pardo planned to distribute to the men under Sergeant Moyano when he reached Chiaha. He opened some nearby packages of shoes and sandals and distributed a pair of leather shoes first to the Caciques from Olamico and Chiaha. He then gave shoes and sandals to both the litter carriage drivers who had accompanied the Caciques. Then, Pardo distributed a pair of shoes and sandals to the 20 soldiers in the Moyano's contingent, as well as to the soldiers who had accompanied him.

Pardo gave his men five days of rest in Olamico, and then, on October 13, they were off to make their way to the Chiefdom of Coosa and then to the silver mines of Zacatecas and San Martín. The whole garrison at Olamico, now christened Fort San Pedro, joined the expedition going south. This included Daniel Almeyda and Juan Martín de Badajoz.

Rather than continue the trail along rivers to Coosa, the Caciques convinced Captain Pardo to take another route over and through the mountains; perhaps by going this way, they suggested, he might discover some gold or silver. Within a day, the soldiers caught sight of the Great Smoky Mountains and began to climb; by the next day they had reached the highest peak. Along the way, Juan Pardo picked up a reddish stone and gave it to Andres Suarez, the miner, and jeweler. Suarez could not test the stone but told Juan Pardo that it looked like the red rocks found near the silver mines in Zacatecas. The next day, the trail descended into a valley with creeks and a river running through it. The name of the Indian town was Chalahume. To Juancinto Taranto, Chalahume reminded him of Córdoba, with the Quadalquivir running through its narrow valley, and his thoughts turned to Solea. He felt her presence within him.

The next day they marched along the river, and by noon they reached the town of Sapato. The men rested here within the palisade walls of the town. Toward sundown, two sentinels posted on watchtowers along the wall heard a loud noise coming from some Indians who had gathered outside of the town. The sentinels reported what they had heard to Juan Pardo, and he put the company on alert.

That evening Rufín, Daniel Almeyda, and Juan Martín found lodging in a house near the palisade wall. While they were sleeping, around midnight, an Indian entered the house and crept up to where Rufín and Daniel were sleeping on platforms against the wall of the house. Daniel was the first to wake-up, and he placed his hand on his knife, ready to plunge it into the Indian. But the man, as he approached Rufín, began whispering his name, as if he knew him, "Rufín, Rufín." Rufín stirred and then woke up. He recognized the man as someone who had been traveling with them since Olamico. He spoke in Cherokee, and Rufín, who had been studying various dialects of Cherokee, managed to understand. The man told Rufín that the Indians of Coosa, Sapato, Chiaha, Olamico, and other towns were banding together and had planned to ambush the Pardo expedition in three places along the trail to Coosa. He offered to tell more if Rufín would manage to convince Captain Pardo to give him an axe. Pardo was told and agreed to this. The man further informed Pardo that the Spaniards were not traveling along the easiest trail to Coosa, which followed the river that Olamico was on. A series of ambushes against the Spaniards had been set up, which would destroy them before they reached Coosa.

In the early morning hours of that night, Daniel found an Indian friend that had accompanied the soldiers, as an interpreter, from Olamico. He spoke both Catawban and Cherokee. This Indian told Daniel that he had heard that Coosa Mico, great chief of Coosa, had let it be known to all, that no one was to give any food to the Spaniards unless they paid for it, and that he and his allies would wage war against the Spaniards. This friend from Olamico also told Daniel that 26 summers ago, when de Soto came through Chiaha, five members of his clan had gone with the soldiers of de Soto.

The friend said, "The people of Coosa and the neighboring towns attacked de Soto and killed him and his men. They enslaved my clansmen; I fear trouble for myself if I have to go there."

Daniel communicated this conversation to Captain Pardo, along with what he had heard from the headman at Napochies that the ruler of Coosa was assembling warriors from dozens of towns to wipe out the Spaniards.

The next morning, Juan Pardo summoned the Cacique of Sapato and asked him to provide him with men to carry their burdens to Coosa. The chief made some excuses and went off looking for burden bearers. He returned with no one, and Pardo observed that, like at Olamico, there were no men from the town of Sapato to be seen. In fact, none of the men that had accompanied them from Olamico and Chiaha were to be seen either. This was confirmation enough for Pardo. He knew a plot and an ambush were being set up.

Juan Pardo called a meeting of his key men and told them what was transpiring. He asked them to vote on continuing with the expedition to Coosa or turning back to Chiaha by the easier river route. The vote was mixed, so Pardo decided to turn back.

It had taken Pardo and his men three days to journey through the mountains from Olamico to Sapato. Now, taking the river trail, which they learned was called The Great Indian Warpath, they reached Chiaha and then Olamico in just two days. Upon arriving, Juan Pardo began to expand the fort. After a few days of work on this project, Juan Pardo left a detachment of 25 men at Fort San Pedro in Olamico and took the balance, about 120 men, back up over the Appalachee Mountains toward Cauchi. It had taken six days to come down the mountains from Cauchi; now, returning up the mountains, it took seven days.

At Cauchi, the Cherokee village set in the gorge of the French Broad River, Pardo laid out the design for another fort. Within three days, they had had it build and named it Fort San Pablo. Captain Pardo left 11 of his troops at Fort San Pablo, including Daniel Almeyda and Juan Martín de Badajoz. Both men, who, on many occasions, had demonstrated to Juan Pardo and Sergeant Moyano their language versatility, were given specific instructions to learn the Cherokee language and its various dialects, and to be vigilant for signs of Indian unrest or unusual movements.

The Pardo expedition rested for a few days at Fort San Pablo in Cauchi, and then on November 1, set out again with a troop size reduced to near 109 men. They proceeded upstream along the French Broad River valley trail, and later at the eastern ridge, down the mountain trail to Joara. From deep in the mountains to the barracks of Fort San Juan, the trek took five days. They arrived in Joara, exhausted, on November 6, 1567. Captain Pardo, perhaps with growing worries of a bad reception at Santa Elena due to the lack of finding the route to Zacatecas or finding gold or silver, authorized Sergeant Moyano and Suarez, the jeweler, to go back to their crystal mine and bring evidence of crystal gems. These two men returned within a few days with a large piece of crystal they had broken off with a pick.

Pardo and all the soldiers stayed about eighteen days in Joara. On November 24, he left Fort San Juan with a garrison of 30 men, including Ruy Gonçalves and Davide Mendes, and proceeded to march due south to observe the famous crystal mine. After seeing the crystal mine, Pardo and company returned to their journey to Santa Elena, but by a long circuitous route making detours to Guatarí and Ylasi on the Yadkin River.

CHAPTER 10

SNAKEBIT

CAUCHI AND CANOSAQUI AUTUMN 1567- SPRING 1568

Daniel and Juan Martín de Badajoz were among those 11 that were assigned to Cauchi, the two having special orders to learn Cherokee and other useful dialects or bits of information. With Daniel came the twelfth immigrant to Cauchi, Immokalee, the daughter of Olamico Orata and Daniel's new wife.

In Cauchi, Immokalee managed to find two small houses together on a hill overlooking the Spaniard's corn storage house. Daniel and Immokalee occupied one house and Juancinto, the other. Housed together in the 20 feet by 20 feet fort were the other nine soldiers, who were all native Spaniards. Most of these soldiers were to some degree jealous of the freedoms that Juan Martin and Daniel Almeyda seemed to be enjoying, but they kept their resentment to themselves. They were afraid of Juan Martin's quick barber's razor, combined with Daniel's sharp tongue and imposing demeanor. Immokalee rapidly made the transition from Creek to Cherokee and was soon gossiping with the women as they washed clothes and fished in the river. One of her new feminine friends was, in fact, not a woman. He dressed as a woman and did all the womanly tasks such as gardening, cooking, cleaning, and dancing at festivals. He told Immokalee that he was the brother of Cauchi Orata. When Daniel expressed astonishment at this acceptance of homosexuality, Immokalee was perplexed.

"What's wrong? Some males are not meant for war. It would be wrong to make them fight. They are more comfortable acting like a woman, making themselves useful and happy doing a woman's work, and some women are happier walking the warpath. Although few and far between, these women are also respected for who they are."

"And what path do you walk, Immokalee?"

"My love, whether war or peace, it's all the same to me. I walk the path you are on. We walk together. You are in my soul. You will never be lonely with me, and I will never be lonely with you."

Daniel loved to hear her talk like this and the sound of those word with her delightful Creek accent gave him the feeling that together they would conquer all obstacles.

Cauchi was not very different from most Cherokee villages nestled on the banks of a river. But with Cauchi, this landscape feature was especially dramatic with mountainous terrain on all sides funneling down to the swift winding river and the gorge it created.

The three of them were in Cauchi no more than two weeks when Immokalee, feeling restless, suggested that they take a canoe trip downriver to the next town, Canosaqui. The autumn morning was brisk and Canosaqui was famous for its hot springs, where many people sought relief from rheumatism, which was called 'the crippler.'

The three individuals paddled together in a stout poplar canoe. The river ride was exhilarating, and they skillfully moved through and around numerous whitewater rapids. After a few hours and not far from their destination, they came to a noisy place in the river signaled by a line of large boulders with a small gateway between them, through which the current rushed down into a cloud of frothy turbulence. With the experience from Suck Creek still fresh in their minds, they decided to portage around this obstacle. They pulled the canoe out of the water, Juancinto taking the bow with Daniel the stern, with Immokalee following. They proceeded up the slope of the forested riverbank. Much of the leaves had already fallen. Each footstep sounded a crunch in the brown and gold ground-covering as the three marched through the brush toward the river trail above.

Suddenly there was a shout, "A la puta!" Juancinto dropped the bow of the canoe and grabbed his ankle.

They watched as a large copperhead slithered away in the rustling leaves. Juancinto had two deep fang holes above his right ankle. Immokalee, reacting quickly, made Daniel remove his leather belt and used it as a tourniquet, tying it at Juancinto's knee. She had Daniel cut into the fang holes with his knife and then she sucked the blood out, spitting in on the ground. After a few minutes of this, she went back down to the riverbank and washed out her mouth.

Immokalee and Daniel proceeded with the portage of the canoe with Juancinto limping behind. His ankle was already starting to swell and turn purple. They put the canoe back into the water beyond the dangerous rapids and within 20 minutes pulled up to the riverbank at the village of Canosaqui on the south side of the river. A crowd of villagers had already gathered. Before Daniel could steer the boat onto the small stony beach, Immokalee was out in the water and asking the curious group of bystanders where the medicine man lived and what was his name.

The crowd pointed to a nearby hill and answered, "Suye'ti, the medicine man, lives on the other side of that hill."

Juancinto limped along, supported on each side by his companions with his arms draped on their shoulders. The house of the shaman stood by itself. The structure had a wood shake roof with wood timber walls, all overshadowed by the bare branches of a large hickory tree, noteworthy due to a 20-foot long lightning strike gash running up the side of the trunk. Immokalee, in a loud but musical voice, inquired at the doorway if this was the house of Suye'ti, the medicine man. The door opened, and a woman's head appeared with a large smile and glistening eyes. Her long curly black hair, pleasantly oiled was streaked with silver, revealing her years of experience. Her demeanor changed when she saw the three standing there with Juancinto slumped in the middle.

"What has happened? If you are looking for Suye'ti, he is here. I am Quhana. He is my father. What can I tell him?"

Without wasting words in Cherokee, Immokalee replied, "Copperhead. About an hour ago."

Quhana re-entered the house and informed her father that two *nokfilakis* and a Creek woman were here from Cauchi. The short man was bitten by a copperhead about an hour ago.

Suye'ti appeared at the door, elderly after seven decades, but still a robust man. His shoulders were slightly bent and his russet skin was deeply creased. His white hair was disheveled and his eyes sad, but what stood out most were many necklaces hanging down from his chest baring the teeth and claws of numerous large animals, birds, and reptiles. On his shoulder perched a large black crow that seemed to want to do more talking than Suye'ti.

Without a word, the old man took Juancinto by the hand and escorted him through the yard to a large bark-less tree trunk lying on the ground, serving both as a seat and examination table. While the crow was complaining, Suye'ti sat Juancinto down at one end of the trunk with Immokalee and Daniel supporting his back. Then the shaman lifted Juancinto's bitten leg up onto the log, stretching it out. Straddling the log and grasping Juancinto's foot, he removed the sandal. The ankle was blotched blue in color and swollen twice its size. The wound revealed fang and knife marks. Suye'ti spat on the wound and began rubbing in his saliva in a circular counter-clockwise fashion. Then he signaled to his daughter to bring him something, and she quickly emerged from the house with a small clay pot.

"What is inside the jar?" Immokalee inquired perhaps impolitely.

"Tobacco leaf juice," Suye'ti answered.

He looked into Juancinto's eyes, and with Immokalee translating, began to chant.

> *Listen! Ha! I am a great ada'nehi (healer)*
> *I will never fail at anything. I will surpass all others.*
> *I am a great healer. Ha!*
> *It is merely a Usu'gi (a small reptile of the copperhead variety)*
> *It has frightened this foreign man; undoubtedly, it has frightened him.*
> *Ha! Instantly I have put the Usu'gi away on the bluff.*
> *Ha! There I compel him to remain.*[8]

Suye'ti looked up at Juancinto and saw he was turning pale, shivering, and perhaps crying.

"What is it you are afraid of?" Suye'ti asked.

Juancinto was near delirium; he muttered, "I am afraid of dying. I hear Atora calling me."

"Where is Atora?" Suye'ti asked.

"She is in the other world, calling me to dance with her."

Rubbing his wound with tobacco juice, Suye'ti assured him, "It is not time for you to go to her yet. Your work here is not done."

"But she saved me from the snake in Lake Iguaque, and then I betrayed her. Atora is calling me to her now with that snake, I know it."

"That may be true, young man, but this I tell you: I see into your soul, and your work here is not done. Between your strength and my strength, we are stronger than Atora and her snakes. All she could muster was a simple copperhead. You will be all right, son; bear with me."

Suye'ti then repeated his first chant. He poured tobacco juice again onto the wound and began to rub it in. He started at the fang bites and rubbed outwards in the same counterclockwise direction. He did these curricular motions four times, mumbling as he went, which were mimicked by the raven on his shoulder. By this time, Immokalee and Quhana were chatting. Quhana informed Immokalee of what her father was doing.

"The rubbing of the snake wound has to be done in a spiral pattern starting on the left and redone four times. Then the air, blown from my father's mouth follows the spiral four times. This is to blow the spirit back over the bluff. The snake is lying on the ground, ready to strike. It is always curled up to the right, and what Suye'ti is doing is uncoiling the snake, taking the energy and aggression out of the animal, and blowing its destructive spirit away. Your friend will survive the snake bite, but it looks like he may have other problems stemming from his past."

"Yes, but I wouldn't know about that," commented Immokalee.

Daniel was eavesdropping on this conversation and understood enough Cherokee to get the gist of the matter. He pulled the women out of Juancinto's earshot and whispered.

"Before we came to this land, Juancinto thought he was cursed because he caused the death or demise of the three women who loved him—one was his wife. His mother-in-law convinced him to start a new life, and I convinced him that he was no longer cursed."

"How did you do that?" both women inquired.

"That is a secret better left unsaid," Daniel replied. "I am sure Juancinto still has ghosts in his past that he has to deal with on occasion, and this experience may help him in doing that."

Then Daniel asked Quhana, "Did your father tell Juancinto that his work here was not done?"

"Yes."

"Why?"

"Sometimes my father can see into the future. I cannot tell you more."

That answer left Daniel both perplexed and assured.

Suye'ti turned to his daughter and told her to take the snake-bitten *nokfilaki* down to the hot springs and sit on the low flat rock and have him dangle his legs in the hot water.

"Don't let him pass out! Keep him talking."

Quhana and Immokalee, one on each side, led Juancinto to the hot spring pool beside the river. They settled on the flat rock as instructed by Suye'ti.

Quhana started the conversation by asking Juancinto what his name was. He began to answer but became tongue-tied with "Ahh . . .Um . . . Ah . . ."

Immokalee answered for him, "His name is Juancinto."

Juancinto, still a little dazed, asserted, "But here I am known as Juan Martín de Badajoz."

"Why do you have two names?" Quhana asked.

"Because I am the only Gypsy on the expedition, so it was easier to change my name from Juancinto Taranto, a Gypsy name, to Juan Martín de Badajoz, a Castellan name."

"What is a 'Gypsy,' and what is wrong with being one?" Quhana inquired.

This topic threw Juancinto back into his days with Atora, and he began to quiver. Quhana put her long thin arm around him, drew him closer, and told him not to worry.

"I have an idea." announced Daniel as he got up and ran to the canoe to fetch Juancinto's guitar. He returned and put the guitar in Juancinto's hands, informing Quhana that she would not know the soul of this Gypsy until she heard him play *palos gitanos* style.

Juancinto took the guitar in his hands and tried to tune it. He could feel numbness in his fingers, so he concentrated on them, moving the fingers back and forth. Quhana took his right hand between her two hands and rubbed it back and forth and blew on it for a full minute and then did the same with his left hand. She smiled broadly and returned his hand and said, "Now try it."

Daniel had positioned himself behind Juancinto with his back touching Juancinto's back to support him. On one side was Immokalee, and on the other was Quhana. Quhana's hand lightly followed the contours of Juancinto's leg, coaxing the poison to leave. Juancinto felt secure, but he did not know where to start. Daniel whispered, "Don't think of Atora. Don't play for her; play for another."

Juancinto closed his eyes, breathed deeply, and let his fingers walk on the strings. Soon he began to play old familiar chord progressions from his Triana neighborhood in Seville. As he played, he heard the clack, clack, clack of steel heels on cobblestone. Then clapping, and Solea's high pitched, imploring voice. He saw the hem of her long skirt whirl by, showing her strong, insistent legs. Looking up, he saw her radiant, smiling face and took heart, slapping the guitar in rhythm with her feet. His fingers fell back to the strings. Solea encouraged him to speed up, but he could not. He looked at her apologetically, and she laughed, threw her hair back to reveal another musician behind her, playing furiously as he stared at Juancinto. It was Quim! His son was now a full-grown man, and better musician than his father. Solea continued to whirl, stomp, and sing at a faster pace. Juancinto was content to accompany Quim with some old riffs he remembered. His fingers began to lose the paralysis of the viper's venom. The piece came to an end with a flourish. There was applause, with romany shouting for more as the scene began to fade.[9]

In Juancinto's head the applause was drowned out by another sound— the roar of rushing water. This was not the sound of the swift-flowing French Broad River before them. No, it was that river sound magnified one thousand times. It was pure current, pure energy. It was the rush of the tremendous turbulence of Iguaçu, churning up the waters of the Paraná into a vapor mist that billowed up to meet the sun. Against the drone of falling waters, he could make out the tiny pinpricks of delicate music, like *ñanduti* lace that Nani used to design.[10] Juancinto echoed the pinpricks with his guitar and recognized them as coming from Nani's Irish harp. There she was in the backdrop of the mighty falls. Behind her were other Guaraní musicians, playing the violin, flute, drum, and dancing. Juancinto laughed and shouted in Guaraní with them. When the music stopped, Nani turned to Juancinto said, "Up beyond these falls, I found my mother and became a mother. Now we will play our '*cante*,'"[11] and she began to sing softly in Castellano accompanied by Juancinto's rasping voice and now invigorated fingers:

Hand in hand
We discover other meadows and other rivers,
Other valleys full of flowers and shady places,
Where we rest and you can always
See yourself in my eyes
Without fear and the trauma of losing yourself.

When the *cante* over, Nani turned to Juancinto and said, "Now rest, Juancinto, your work is not over." Then Nani disappeared into the falling waters of Iguaçu.

Daniel, Immokalee, and Quhana heard and watched Juancinto and were as entranced as he was. His face was now wet with tears. They all cried, and Juancinto collapsed in Quhana's lap, exhausted, happy, and feeling purified.

Daniel and Immokalee spent that night in Canosaqui and the next day walked the river trail back to Cauchi.

The medicine man, Suye'ti, ordered Juancinto to stay and to recuperate. He passed the next few days with Quhana, re-living his life's story at her insistence—his "*cante.*" In exchange, she revealed her story to him, which he tried to put to music.

Juancinto remarked to Quhana that in his vision at the hot springs, Solea and Nani came to him, but not Atora. And he wondered why.

Quhana said that her father told her that Atora was there.

"No, she wasn't!"

"Yes, she was there in the form of the copperhead that bit you to cure you of your ghosts. Father said, Atora was powerful! If she had really wanted to harm you, she would have been a rattlesnake, or the great serpent, Uktena."

Once again, Juancinto felt that pull, that same longing that had stirred in him when he took his sister, Giralda, to La Gitanilla's dance class and had first witnessed Solea Ballesteros. He had thought that he had finally outgrown, or become immune to, these sexual disturbances and moved on to the level of the wise and passionless. Apparently, Fate led him to the hot springs for the cure, and, no doubt, for the time being he was in the hands of a competent physician. But was not three times enough? What life lesson could be learned from a fourth episode with love? Perhaps, as Suye'ti had said, "His work here was not yet done." But he was a grown man with worlds of experience, why was he acting like a youth when in Quhana's presence?

He observed her closely. She could not be more different from his other three loves. She was the opposite. He was 43 years old, an "old man" past his prime. She was ten years younger, and most would say, still in her prime. He was short, square, and wiry. He was bow-legged, and he rocked as he walked.

She was three inches taller, and there would be many that would suggest that Quhana was lanky, with long and thin legs, arms, and neck. Even her breasts were slim in keeping with the balance of her appearance. Immobile, you would consider her gaunt and awkward, but in motion, although her strides were long, she had grace and balance. She glided through space and did not rock and waddle as he did. Whereas his extremities were swarmed with thin clouds of black hair over olive skin, her smooth, deep copper skin sported intricate geometric designs often found on the local pottery.

But, most important to Juancinto was this: even though she moved with an innate grace balanced by determination, *she did not seem to be a natural dancer*, like Solea or Atora, nor an artist or musician of the caliber of Nani. Although true, Quhana, like Nani, was a healer. From her father, she had developed a keen observation of the human world and its natural environs, as well as the world above and that underneath. At root, she was loving, and she was a pearl of practical wisdom.

Quhana's hair was not straight-falling like most women of her tribe. Their hair was the one thing that Quhana and Juancinto had in common: both had curly, unruly black hair streaked with silver. With her hair tied up, she still had natural curls over her ears, with long fingers cultivating those curls. Juancinto could easily imagine her as if she were a princess at a Gypsy King's wedding in Algarve or Andalusia.

But what fascinated Juancinto most about Quhana's presence was not her hair or inquisitive eyes, but her mouth. It relaxed naturally into a pondering pout with her lips bowed downward, giving rise to dimples on each cheek. To Juancinto's eyes, the pondering frown was a form of yearning, or better yet, a cross between yearning and knowing, which captured Juancinto's heart.

He wanted to kiss that pouting mouth and transform it so easily into a broad smile with gleaming teeth and brilliant laughter.

***

"I was seven years old when de Soto came through. Even I could see that everything changed. Oh yes, after the *nokfilakis* came through and were later defeated, our lives eventually settled back down to something like normal. But even then, our world contained the lingering memory of men with beards and their shiny armor, pipes that shot fire as they rode huge swift animals, and the lingering notion that they could someday return. These soldiers marched through, accompanied by thousands of warriors from strange tribes employed to do their dirty work. Herds of pigs, which we had never seen, as vast as a ballgame field, trampled our crops, but the worst were the war dogs. I still dream about them, although I never saw one mangle a body.

"They came through and rested for the night. They took all our corn, supplies, and everything they judged to be of value. But they did not kill or enslave anyone or force us to be their burden bearers. That only began in the following weeks when they arrived in Olamico.

"We soon recovered, and my life was good with my mother and father. My mother was loving, and she kept me busy by teaching me to keep a home, and I was the son my father did not have— but that it did not bother him a bit. I accompanied him on most of his foraging trips, as well as other strange trips. He never expected me to be a warrior; instead, he trained me to be a healer, like himself.

"By the time I was of marrying age I was not interested in any of the boys outside of my clan. Here in Canosaqui, the boys were not attracted to me. My father even inquired in Cauchi, Tocae, and the surrounding area with no results. So, things went on like this for about five years. I did not mind, but by the time I had 22 years my parents were desperate for a suitor.

"And then Pasque came to Canosaqui. He was my age and the son of a powerful family in Tanasqui, the first walled town on the river, and a day's canoe trip from here on the way to Olamico. Early on, Pasque's mother had seen in him the makings of a medicine man. She had raised him as such, almost against her husband's wishes. Pasque was well versed in the healing arts and conjuring by his mother and the local shaman. I don't know whether my father lured him to Canosaqui with the prize of marrying me, or whether he came of his own accord. Anyway, he showed up one day to study with the famous Suye'ti, and my father took him in to be his apprentice and possible son-in-law.

"Pasque was not a bad looking man. Mind you, he was not a warrior, and he had something of his mother in him, something that was not good, but I didn't see it at the time. I welcomed the opportunity to please my parents, and at first Pasque and I seemed to be a natural fit. We had been brought up for the same healing ends. As a woman of 22 years, I had bound-up my sexual desires until then, and they were ready to explode. In our intimate time, Pasque, understanding my repression, took advantage of his knowledge of me and the world to create cloudbursts of sexual energy around us. We both knew enough of herbs and cycles and conjury to avoid pregnancy, so that was not a problem. By the first Green Corn Ceremony, we were married. It was only after that that I noticed certain things in his character that disturbed me.

"Pasque once told me that his aunt told him that when he was an infant, before he could remember, his mother fed him fermented corn hominy instead of mother's milk. That was so strange, and I wondered what his baby dreams were like. I mentioned this to my father and he was very concerned. I asked what the problem was, and he said, 'That is what a witch feeds her infant son to give him special powers.'"

"Pasque would often ask about my father's powers. 'Could he fly? Could he shape-shift?' I told him, 'No, not to my knowledge.' Pasque seemed disappointed, as if he were wasting his time being in Canosaqui.

"Once I found him in some swampy land collecting arrowhead root. He made a concoction from this plant and fasted for seven days only drinking this liquid. He said that doing this would enable him to change into any animal, not only in this world, but also in the Upper World and in the Lower World. He said that he would be able to fly, and dive under the ground.

"I could have accepted all this and lived with Pasque, the great shaman, but Pasque, I came to believe, was not a good man, some say, not even human."

"How's that?" Juancinto inquired.

"We have a word in Cherokee, 'dugu:gho: d^.' It means straight, upright, righteous, true, just. A man with this is a man with Soul, Feeling, or Heart, as we say. There is another kind of man or woman who is 'v:ne:gu: tso: d^.' These people are heartlessly evil. They are not born as such but re-make themselves into something which is no longer human but heartless and evil.

"I soon realized that I did not want to have children with this man, so I kept to my herbs, techniques, and claimed to be barren.

"After about three years, our relationship—our marriage fell apart. It started when he began to urge me to have a sexual relationship with a friend of his, a married man. He said, 'Just to see if I was really barren, or if it was him?' I had no attraction to this man, and indeed, his wife was one of my best friends. I thought this was an absurd idea.

"Then, soon after he began talking like this, I found him in his secret place in the forest. I had gone there quietly to watch him because I thought something was going on. He was practicing a ritual. He was invoking the Blue Hawk because the Blue Hawk always brings trouble, separating lovers, and spoiling their souls for one another. He referred to himself as a 'white man,' meaning that he was happy, fortunate, attractive, irresistible, and never lonely. He called to the Blue Hawk, saying that he was paying him with re-made Blue Tobacco. The Blue Hawk was invoked and alighted midway between Pasque's so-called 'friend' and his wife, Suya, my friend, who Pasque desired for himself."

"'Now! I have spoiled their Souls. They have at once become separated.'"

"Pasque continued with the invocation. 'I am a white man. My good sperm shall never allow any feeling of loneliness. This white woman is of the Paint Clan, and she is called Suya. We shall constantly turn her soul over as we go toward the Sunland. I am a white man. Here, now, her soul has attached itself to mine. Let her eyes in their sockets be forever watching for me. There is no loneliness where my body is.'"[11]

Quhana said she was disgusted, and soon, indeed, her marriage was broken, and Pasque had an affair with Suya.

"By now, my father was no longer suffering any illusions about Pasque."

"What do you mean by 'no illusions?'" asked Juancinto.

"My father saw deeper into Pasque than I did. He noticed that Pasque was taking more of an interest in people who were dying. Now, this is not strange for an abitious young medicine man. Pasque was rarely home at night, particularly if someone in the surrounding settlements was on their deathbed. On the outside, he asserted that he was protecting their hearts from being secretly devoured by witches. But he was usually the last person holding the hand of the deceased as their soul passed.

"And then one day, about five years ago, Pasque just disappeared. He went out foraging on the mountain and never returned. Many bands of hunters between here and Tanasqui set out looking for the body, but none was ever found. I had always felt that my father knew something. Three years ago, after the shock of his disappearance had subsided, I asked my father to tell me, even if he had to go into the Other Worlds, the real reason why my husband had vanished."

He said, "No need to go into the Other Worlds. I know what happened to him. I killed him. I cut off his head."

"Why?"

"He was well on his way to becoming a Raven Mocker.[12]

"How did you know?"

"I watched him closely and on more than one occasion I saw him capture the soul of a dying person as it was leaving the body."

Quhana then asked, "I thought Raven Mockers sucked the hearts out of dying people without cutting into their bodies?"

Suye'ti replied, "Quhana, let me ask you something?"

"Okay."

"Has the Council ever ordered that a corpse, suspected of being tampered with by a witch, be cut open to see if the heart is still there?"

"No. I don't think so."

"You're right. It is because the heart is still there. It's the energy of the heart, the soul, that they are after to extend their lives and give them special powers. Raven Mockers can see this energy and develop ways to capture it as it tries to escape the dying body."

"What did you do with Pasque's body?"

"We wrapped him in deerskins with large pockets for heavy stones, and the head— tied it with good rope and sank it in the deepest part of the river, up toward Cauchi, where Uktena lives."

"So, you had help?"

"Of course."

"Who helped you?"

"You don't need to know. But now that you know the truth, you will promise never to tell anyone in the village or hereabouts."

"I promise, Father."

"Good. Among people who understand, Pasque's killing is an open secret. We are all glad he is gone, and we know why. Even in Tanasqui, they did not make a grand effort to find him. The Council and the family do not want their names associated with a Raven Mocker."

***

Juancinto and Quhana became inseparable after his ordeal with the snakebite.

Daniel received permission for Juan Martín de Badajoz to remain in Canosaqui to study the Cherokee language, and medicinal herbs with Suye'ti's family as well as to be a listening outpost for what was happening downriver. Quhana and Juancinto resided in the compound with Suye'ti and Sanapa, Quhana's mother, but because the winter season following Juancinto's arrival was one of the coldest in memory, Juancinto and Quhana passed most to their time in the *"asi,"* or sweat lodge, by the garden in the back of Suye'ti's house. The *"asi"* was large enough for them both, ten feet by ten feet and four feet high with a small opening and chimney hole in the middle. It was dug into the ground with a floor, walls, and a ceiling lined with logs and earth covering everything. Over the floor were piles of bearskins. After adjustments made for the smoke, it was warm and cozy.

When the snows were deepest, Quhana and Juancinto would spend whole days in the *"asi"* without coming out. During the winter, Quhana helped Juancinto with his Cherokee, and he with her Castellano. Quhana developed her *"cante,"* and Juancinto put it to music. Quhana related to Juancinto all the Cherokee myths so many times over that he memorized them and put the ancient stories and prayers to music with his guitar.

As harsh as the winter was, an early spring was the reward for having endured it. By mid-March, many people in pain started coming to the hot springs seeking relief. Juancinto and Quhana were there to address "the crippler" and other maladies with massage, music, and prayers, supplemented with melodious tales from the mountains of the Cherokee and ancient myths from around the round world.

By April 1, new life had begun to stir in Quhana's womb. Juancinto asked Quhana to marry him, the ceremony to be at the late-summer Green Corn Ceremony. Life in paradise had turned out well for Juancinto.

Chapter 11

Unrest in Joara

Winter 1567-156

Davide and Ruy heard the rumor that Juan Pardo and the men were at the top of the mountain and would be marching into Joara in a few days. They were excited at the possibility that they were to see their "blood brothers" after an absence of almost a year. Davide wondered out-loud, "What tales we have to tell Daniel and Juancinto and what stories they will have for us!", but, on second thought he considered, 'Captain Pardo only left here less than two months ago. Could they have found the route to Zacatecas and be back so soon?'

Ruy commented, "Too soon. Something went wrong." But as the troops marched in through the western neighborhoods and entered the barracks plaza, Ruy noted, "They all seem to be intact, no fatalities or wounded."

Ruy saw a friend and asked, "Have you seen Daniel Almeyda and Juan Martín de Badajoz?"

The friend replied, "They were assigned to Fort San Pablo in Cauchi at the top of the mountain. They are supposed to be learning Cherokee there. Daniel is now married to the daughter of the Chief of Olamico. All three are living in Cauchi."

Ruy, reflecting on Daniel and Juancinto, laughed and said "Why does that not surprise me!" and Davide joked, "Why are you back so soon? Are your pockets full of that Zacatecas silver?"

"No, we never really got out of the mountains. We rescued Sergeant Moyano at a place called Olamico and enlarged the fort there. That is the place where Daniel married the daughter of the chief. From Olamico, we marched for a few days south through the mountains toward the big Chiefdom of Coosa. We got as far as the Creek town of Sapato. There we learned that three thousand Indians were waiting to ambush us like they did de Soto. Juan Pardo didn't like the odds, what with no horses and all, so we turned around and came back. And here we are."

"What are Pardo's plans?" Ruy asked. "Do you know? It was hard enough here two months ago, with 125 extra mouths to feed. Everyone complained. And now you're back, and it's winter. You'll eat up all the stores in a month, and the Indians won't put up with it. They will refuse to feed you."

"They will have to." was the reply. "We have the gun powder. Anyway, I hear we will only be here for two or three weeks, and we'll return with Captain Pardo to Santa Elena."

'*Good riddance,*'thought Davide. '*Life had been good for the past year with just ten of us strangers for a thousand Joarans to put up with. A certain balance was achieved; now, the balance is threatened.*'

Joara Mico saw things in a different light.

'*It was true that two months ago when Captain Pardo passed through with his 125 men, they only stayed for two nights. But it was just after the Green Corn Ceremony, and Pardo took more than the Spanish King's share of the new corn harvest. And now they are back! They avoided the ambush. I must tell him that my hunters have let it be known that they cannot—will not supply meat for all these soldiers.*'

That night, Juan Pardo met with Joara Mico with Erbani and Rufín present, as translators. Pardo informed the Mico that he and most of the new arrivals would be staying for no more than 20 days and then returning to Santa Elena. In the meantime, he would keep his men busy constructing another barracks and an enclosed kitchen.

Joara Mico replied, "That is good, but my hunters have refused to hunt for you for nothing in return, and I am sure that my builders will feel the same way. We don't need any more glass bead necklaces and chisels. If you give me three axe-heads I will supply your men with meat, but it will be only deer and turkey. No bear. And we will keep the skins. Now, for four more metal knives, we will help build your new barracks and kitchen."

Juan Pardo answered, "That is a hard bargain, Joara Mico. I can supply you with the axe heads, but that's the last of my supply of trade tools. No more knives. Will you take ten pairs of Spanish sandals in return for help with the barracks and kitchen?"

"No. I cannot do that."

"Well then, I will supply you with the axe-heads in exchange for the hunters, but we will have to build the new structures ourselves, without your help."

"As you wish." replied the Mico.

"Yes, that will be our arrangement for now, Joara Mico, but let me remind you of something. You swore allegiance to the King of Spain and the Holy Church. King Phillip is the Mico of Micos, and you here, in Joara, are but his subjects. Just as the settlements of Clara and Adini, and so many others, pay tribute to you, you must pay tribute to King Phillip. We are warriors for King Phillip. We are the King's principle men here in this land. Just as I asked you to build a storehouse for corn, which you did as a tribute to your king and Ruler, now I ask you, in the name of the king, for smaller things, and you want to bargain? We are here to help you and protect you and raise the souls of the people to recognize Jesus Christ."

"I don't need your protection, Captain Pardo," replied the Chief.

Pardo responded, "Today, you want to bargain as in the marketplace. Tomorrow you will be grateful for our presence and pay tribute."

"We shall see." answered the Mico.

"Oh, and one more thing, Joara Mico, I almost forgot: Adelantado Menéndez, who is the King's principal man at Santa Elena, told me to reorganize the barracks and garrison here and to start enforcing what he calls "Ordinance 137." That is a ruling from Madrid that says that no Indians can be allowed inside the fort. Now, your women do our cooking and will continue, even with our new kitchen, and your men can come in and out of the barracks as they please. I cannot stop that. But I must not allow your people to enter our actual fort with the moat and the palisade walls with our storehouse inside. Do you understand that? Is that clear?"

"Yes, I understand," replied Joara Mico, with a curious look on his face.

Joara Mico thought to himself, *'It is true, what Coosa Mico says, that the Spaniards intend to stay here, dominate us, and turn us into their slaves.'*

***

On November 24, after spending 18 days in Joara, Captain Pardo began a slow journey back to Santa Elena. He left 30 additional men to augment the 10 previously stationed at the garrison at Fort San Juan. Ruy and Davide were relieved to hear that they could stay in Joara. In charge of the garrison was Ensign Alberto Villamar. He was ordered by Juan Pardo to conserve the friendship of the chiefs and to govern all four forts in the region; the forts in Olamico, Cauchi, and in Guatari, as well as Fort San Juan in Joara.

Very soon it was evident that the Spaniards would have to supply their own firewood for cooking and heating. This kept some men occupied while others kept busy playing cards and developing new skills like curing tobacco and fermenting wild grapes and passionflower fruit into wine.

Captain Pardo, with his remaining troupe of 79 men, first marched southeast to investigate the crystal mines earlier explored by Sergeant Moyano near the town of Yssa on the South Catawba River fork. After a week of this activity, and with a bag of crystals, Pardo decided to march northeast toward the Chiefdom of Guatarí on the Yadkin River. It took a week marching cross country to arrive there. Pardo and his men spent three weeks in the large town of Guatarí, which he renamed "Cuidad de Salamanca." They built a larger fort there with a chapel and named the structure Fort Santiago. Captain Pardo garrisoned an additional 16 men at this fort under the command of Corporal Lucas de Canicares. Of note in his parting instruction to the Corporal, Pardo insisted that Lucas de Canicares swear, probably to satisfy the priest, Montero, not to allow women into the fort at night. No other of Pardo's garrison commanders were ordered to take such an oath baring Indian women from the barracks at night.

Augmenting the garrison at Fort Santiago with the additional 16 soldiers left a total of 19 soldiers at Guaratí. Pardo and now 67 soldiers, marched south to arrive at the town of Aracuchi on the Catawba River. Here Pardo sent Sergeant Moyano with a detachment of men downriver to Canos, while he and the rest of the troupe detoured due east, journeying for a few days to reach the large town of Ylasi, on the Yakin River. Pardo rested here for four days and then marched southwest through swamps for a week to rendezvous with Sergeant Moyano at

Canos. They stayed there for a few weeks and built Fort San Tomás, but they did not man the fort in Canos or stock it with munitions or supplies. Perhaps this was because Pardo had heard reports of a rebellion near Orista, or perhaps it was because he needed the extra hands to carry corn sacks from Canos and Guiomae to Santa Elena. After proceeding along the trail by the Catawba River to Guiomae, they then marched with corn sacks two days across swamps to Cacao and were met by friendly Indians from Orista. The soldiers and Indians then journeyed for two more days and came to the town of Ahoya, located 25 miles north of Santa Elena. Juan Pardo had hoped to build a fort and a house at Ahoya, but when he arrived, he discovered that the people of Ahoya had murdered a Spanish Corporal because they were tired of being commanded to ferry supplies in their canoes back and forth to Santa Elena. The Cacique of Ahoya had been imprisoned in Santa Elena, and the villagers had burned the village and dispersed into the dense forest.

The Cacique of Orista, Rufín's father-in-law, who had been traveling with the party from Cacao, offered to have a new fort built in his village, and promised to keep canoes ready to comply with the needs of the Spanish. The troups and corn were transported by canoe to Orista. The corn was stored in a large building owned by the chief, and the next day Juan Pardo ordered his men to start building a strong house and a fort, which was named "*Fort Nuestra Señora.*" The town of Orista was renamed "*Buena Esperanza.*"[13] Pardo designated a Corporal and 12 soldiers to be garrisoned at the new fort.

Soon after arriving at Orista, the Captain got word from Santa Elena that the food supply was severely depleted, and there may not be enough food for even 50 of his men in two months. This prompted Captain Pardo to send 30 of his remaining men back north up the Catawba River to Canos to man Fort San Tomás. Pardo then convened a meeting of all the Oratas and headmen of the villages in the area. He gave them all gifts and instructed them to grow corn for the storehouse in Orista and to treat well the soldiers stationed at Fort Nuestra Señora. He told them they were to obey Orista Orata, who would be the chief over them. Then, hearing that a nearby chief had a house full of corn for the Spaniards, he sent 3 men to Guando Orata to gather the corn. When all this was done, on the morning of March 1, 1568, the Captain, with his remaining 21 men, left the new town of Buena Esperanza and paddled canoes to Santa Elena, arriving at the wood-plank dock at three o'clock in the afternoon.

Captain Pardo reported to Adelantado Menéndez that, no, he did not find the route to Zacatecas beyond the mountains, and if he had gone on he might have lost all his men in a massive ambush at the hands of the Creek Indians. No, he did not discover gold or silver, but he did find a crystal mine and he produced a bag of crystals. As it was, he built four small forts and a larger fort and chapel at Guatarí. At each fort, he stationed a contingent of men to be fed and supplied by the local population. He did all of this without suffering a single Spanish casualty, and the only Indians to lose their lives were those that Moyano slaughtered at Chisca.

CHAPTER 12

COOSA MICO

COOSA VILLAGE, OLAMICO VILLAGE EARLY APRIL 1568

For the past 13 moons, messengers had been circulating between Creek, Cherokee, and Catawba towns, updating the various Micos and Oratas throughout the mountains and across the foothills about the ongoing activities of the Spaniards. Warriors from all the tribes from the Coosawattee and the French Broad Rivers in the west, to the Catawba and Yadkin River in the east, were looking to Coosa Mico for leadership in confronting the Spaniards.

It was common knowledge that some 26 years in the past, the nobility of Coosa Chiefdom had suffered cruelty and humiliation at the hands of Hernando de Soto. Coosa Mico was only 26 years old at the time. The friendly de Soto lured him into a meeting and took him and his principle men as hostages in chains and iron collars. The Spaniards demanded women and porters. The people of Coosa fled into the woods. Many were captured and put in collars and chains. Coosa Mico was eventually released by de Soto, but his beloved sister was not, and he never saw her again.

Since those days, Coosa had recovered and even prospered. The Chiefdom had regained its power, and it was now the time for justice and revenge.

It had been 4 moons since Pardo had turned back at Sapato with only 145 men. Coosa Mico, remembered de Soto. He speculated, *'Pardo will most likely return with hundreds on horseback, with armor, swords, crossbows and dogs, followed by thousands of mercenary Indians. But then if Pardo has so many soldiers, why has he left only a handful of men in the five forts that he has built. It has been 4 moons and nothing has transpired, If I had known that the Spaniards were so weak and over-extended I would have attacked last winter at Sapato and wiped them out.'*

Coosa Mico called for his War Chief and told him to send messengers to Olamico, Cauchi, Joara, Guatari, and Canos with the following instructions to be delivered to the Micos and Oratas, "Organize your warriors and be ready to receive Creek and Cherokee warriors from the mountains. Starting at Olamico, on the night of the next full moon, in 20 days from this day, all the houses and forts of the Spaniards are to be burned to the ground, and every '*nokfilacki'* is to be killed. It will start in Olamico and the remaining forts in Cauchi, Joara, Guatarí, and Canos will suffer the same fate."

The runners were dispatched and returned within 12 days, confirming to Coosa Mico that preparations were being made for the moonlight massacres starting at Olamico. On dispatching the runners, Coosa Mico immediately ordered his Gueza, his War Chief, to assemble 500 warriors from Coosa and its surrounding towns and proceed to Tasqui, Chalahume, Sapato, Coste, and Chiaha; he would go to all the towns between Coosa and Olamico, and enlist a war party at each town. These war parties each were instructed to proceed silently to the region of Olamico, contact Gueza and coordinate under his command for the destruction of the fort and its soldiers.

A few days before the full moon date, Coosa Mico was carried on a litter to a mountain perch within a few miles of Olamico, there to experience the first-hand satisfaction of revenge against the people who had kidnapped his sister.

CHAPTER 13

INEBRIATION

JOARA
EARLY APRIL 1568

Thome de Paniagua and Matheo Espadera were young men raised in wine county along the upper Duero River west of Zamora, Spain. Tired of tending the vineyards, picking, and processing the grapes, and, frankly, longing for the adventure they had never had, they signed on together for the Menéndez-Pardo expedition to La Florida after seeing a poster in a Zamora tavern in early 1566. As luck would have it, their original deployment to the new garrison at Fort San Juan had not changed, meaning that now, in the early spring of 1568, they had resided in Joara for over 14 months.

What had changed during the past year was that the original garrison in Joara of 30 men had decreased to 10 after Sergeant Moyano, the commanding officer of the fort, took 20 men and went to Chisca and then on to Olamico waiting for Pardo to rescue him. He and the bulk of the garrison were gone for about seven months. Now, with the return of Pardo and Moyano in November of the past year, the garrison at Fort San Juan had grown from 10 to 40 soldiers, with the rest of the troups returning to Santa Elena with Pardo and Moyano.

During those seven months when there were only 10 soldiers at the Fort, Thome and Matheo adjusted to the peaceful pace of life in Joara by developing a hobby. Just as their comrades, Ruy Gonçalves, with his ball game team, and Davide Mendes with local medicine, Thome and Mateo had concentrated on turning wild grapes into wine.

During the spring and summer of the first year they had located and cultivated patches of wild grapes. When ripe, they harvested the grapes and fermented them with yeast stolen from the supply room in the fort. All this was done with the help of an Indian friend and accomplice named Jueca, who had a cabin about two leagues upstream on the San Juan River north of Joara. On the cabin floor, the wine was kept in large Spanish olive jars confiscated from the kitchen and large ceramic pots supplied by Jueca. To simulate the flavor of oak barrels, the winemakers placed wood chunks from various oak trees into the fermenting brew.

The wine was ready to drink just as Captain Pardo and Sergeant Moyano returned from the mountains with 109 men in tow, but Matheo and Thome thought better about introducing it at that time. They could have divested the expanded garrison of all the extra pocket change, but where could they spend their proceeds?

By early December, the garrison was reduced to a less chaotic 40 soldiers, but still the winemakers wisely decided to keep their secret to themselves. At Christmas, Thome and Matheo celebrated the holiday with Jueca at his cabin with a few large olive jars of their intoxicating beverage. The wine was judged good enough, and their private festival was celebrated until all three celebrants passed out, arising in the cold morning with hangovers.

In the spring of 1568, Thome and Mateo's wine-making venture was no longer a closely held secret, but more of a widely spread rumor. Still, the winemakers were resolved to keep their bodega, at least for the time being, limited to their own private consumption and that of their close friends. However, in a card game late one night with Domingo Calero, Thome, having already gambled away all his current possessions, was faced with losing six months of deferred salary. The pressure was on. Domingo Calero was a notorious bully at the center of a ring of miscreant soldiers who roamed now around Joara like a group of thugs in a poor Seville neighborhood, looking for trouble and amusement at the expense of any weaker entity unfortunate enough to be in their path. Under the circumstances, the equivalent to six months Thome's of wages turned out to be six olive jars of wine.

Avante was the younger sister of Ayo, the promising young warrior, and captain of the ball team. Shortly after turning 15 years old, Avante began to pester her older neighbor, Xequina, to allow her to accompany her and Vara to the Spanish plaza and outdoor kitchen. The common worry in her clan was that Avante was early to ripen for her age, both physically and emotionally, and the concern among Avante's family and friends was that this feature and her quest for experience would get her into trouble, especially with the extra Spaniards in the town.

Avante had always looked up to Xequina, as a model of comportment, even though Xequina was four years her senior. Avante had witnessed Xequina choose Ruy, the ball-playing soldier, over her brother Ayo. She thought, '*What courage that took…and love.*' Avante did not necessarily want to follow Xequina's example, but she did want to broaded her horizon and exert herself as did Xequina. She badgered her mother and went to the house of her brother, Ayo, now living with his new wife in the Paint Clan neighborhood. Avante was relentless in pressing her will, until finally, her mother and brother gave in and allowed her go to the town center and work at the open kitchen at the garrison, but only under the wings and supervision of Vara and Xequina.

Avante worked a few hours each day in the Spanish plaza doing various chores under the watchful eyes for Xequina and Vara. She had followed this routine for two winter moons, and now it was spring. The songbirds had returned, the trees along the creeks were greening, and clothes could be shed to avoid sweat and to allow the new sun and air to warm and refresh the skin. Early on, Avante's roaming eyes had settled on Juan Lopez Sanchez, a stout, good-natured lad from Andalucía, who had just turned nineteen. Juan hardly had a beard, but he did have long, straight, silky black hair that flowed behind him when he ran. Initially, for a couple of weeks, Juan and Avante played a game of stare-and-hide until Juan finally mustered the courage to make verbal contact. Juan used some of the few phrases in Catawban he had learned, "Hello, I am called Juan. What is your name?"

"I am Avante," she replied with a blush.

Juan next exhausted his Catawban vocabulary with, "You're beautiful."

Avante, not knowing how to respond to this, turned on her moccasins and walked off, looking back briefly to smile at Juan.

Juan Lopez Sanchez, being the youngest of the contingent of Spanish soldiers and feeling somewhat vulnerable, had been, from the time of the trip across the Atlantic in need of a protector and guardian. Domingo

Calero gladly seized the opportunity to play this role. Calero had begun training Juan Sanchez to be one of his men, but at this stage, Juan was more of an apprentice on the fringe of Calero's power group than a key player. Calero had observed Juan's approaches to Avante, and for lack of anything better to do, decided to facilitate this interaction. In the storehouse within the Fort, Domingo Calero had managed to find and lift from a bag containing miscellaneous trinkets, a glass bead neckless.

"Here, give this to your sweetheart, Sanchez, and ask her to be your teacher of the Catawban tongue."

When offered, Avante took the necklace and said, "Yes. And I want to speak Castellano. You teach?"

Juan responded with a happy affirmation, "Yes! We will learn each other's language."

Next, Avante introduced Juan to Vara and asked Vara to work out with Juan a private place for their language instruction.

Vara relayed to Juan, "She will meet you here tomorrow after she finishes work in the kitchen. You can walk her toward her home up the creek to a place where you can study speaking in each other's tongues. Do you understand?"

"Yes. I will be here tomorrow," responded Juan.

As soon as she got home that afternoon, Avante hid the necklace for no one to see or have an opinion about, not her mother, not Ayo or her even her neighbor Xequina. Later that evening, Avante went to the house of Xequina and asked her friend and mentor to teach her ten words in Castellano. This, thought Avante, would give them something to talk about and avoid silence.

The next day, after her work in the kitchen, Avante led Juan up the path beside Warrior Creek. The trail was shaded by the new foliage from large trees growing along the creek's bank. Beyond the leafy shade on both sides of the creek were naked fields basking in the afternoon sun. Covering the ground was last season's rotting corn husks. Here and there, villagers were busy preparing the soil for receiving the seeds of this year's crop.

About a half-mile up the creek, and halfway to her village, Avante stopped at a well shaded clearing with a bench beside the creek. The place was good for fishing or watching bathers in the deeper waters of the fishing hole. Straddling the pool was the trunk of a fallen poplar tree, now bark-less and wide enough to use as a bridge to walk across. Avante stopped and sat down on the fishing bench and motioned Juan to sit beside her. She began with the words that Xequina had taught her, knowing enough pronouns and verbs to construct a few crude sentences. The game was simple: for every sentence in Castellano, which Avante could construct, Juan had to learn the equivalent in Catawban. The game was a success with Juan, inspiring Avante not to miss an opportunity to learn new words from Xequina or Vara.

On one unusually hot mid-spring afternoon, Avante proposed that they sit on the log crossing the creek to take advantage of a slight breeze following the water. Perched on the log over the stream, they played their game of matching phrases. Now, for fun, Avante suggested that the penalty for not being able to match a phrase in the other's tongue would be a tumble off the log into the water. Soon they were both in the stream, playing and laughing. Like this, the two developed a certain easy familiarity, which naturally led to a deepening affection.

They used their expanding vocabulary to widen the horizon of natural interest in each other and themselves. At the end of every session by the fishing bench, Juan would walk with Avante along the path to her neighborhood. They would stop in a grove of trees on the outskirts of the village and say good-bye. Avante was never shy, and her intent to push boundaries moved from saying good-bye to kissing good-bye, but only when the couple judged they were alone.

None of this escaped the attention of Domingo Calera and his cohorts. Domingo looked for opportunities in everything that transpired, including the innocent liaison between young Juan Sanchez and a 15-year-old Indian girl. Calera had also just won six olive jars of homemade wine.

One warm, moonlit evening, Juan and Avante arranged to meet at the fishing bench. Avante slipped out of her bed when her parents were asleep, and Juan let it be known at the barracks that he was going out for some romantic activity. Domingo suggested, "In that case, you should carry a jar of new wine to make your escapade more fruitful." Calera expressed the belief that Juan's young girlfriend had probably never tasted wine, and she would surely like it.

Juan took the jar and presented it to Avante when he met her at the bench. At first, the taste was so bitter and disagreeable that Avante spat it out of her mouth. But, as Juan was drinking it, she would too. The more she drank, the better it tasted and felt. There was laughter and a looseness that led to touching and kissing. Soon, the jar was empty.

At about this time, Domingo Calera appeared with two other soldiers and more jars of wine. Between the five of them, they quickly drank one jar and Domingo then proposed that they continue the party by setting a campfire in a forest on the other side of the creek. All agreed that this was a good idea, but only Domingo had the balance to cross the creek on the log bridge. The rest fell off the log and emerged from the creek wet.

Domingo led the group across a cornfield into the forest. They climbed a small hill to a large rock outcropping with a flat surface. The two soldiers went looking for dry kindling, which Domingo assembled, and with the help of a piece of flint and a steel nail, sparked a fire that developed into a bonfire. The men shed most of their clothes to dry near the fire. Domingo coaxed Avante to remove her leather blouse to dry by the fire, urging her to keep warm with more wine and Juan's embraces. Avante obliged, and by the end of the third wine jar, she passed out. Juan was not far behind.

Domingo and his two companions then proceeded to have their way with the unconscious Avante.

At first light, with the sound of early songbirds, Juan awoke with the thought that Avante's people would be looking for her since they stayed out all night. He rolled over to find Avante's naked body, still asleep, beside him. Juan saw blood between her thighs and began to reconstruct what he could remember of the night before. He knew that however drunk he might have been, he had not abused Avante. Domingo and his men had raped her!

He gathered her leather garments which lay by the now smoldering campfire and placed the dry clothes over her. He lay down next to her and put his arm under her neck, drawing himself closer to her. He whispered her name in her ear repeatedly until her eyelids began to flutter and open. At first, she had a blank stare, and then she felt her bruised groin with her hand. She lifted her hand to her face and stared at the blood on her fingers. Not waiting for a reaction from Avante, Juan launched into a sorrowful monologue in Castellano about how sorry he was that he let this happen, that he was passed out before the others took advantage of her, that he would report this to Ensign Villamar, that he was so ashamed that he did not protect her, and that he would have revenge against Domingo and the others.

Avante understood none of this. She could only perceive his emotions, the sound of his voice and gestures of his limbs, all of which seemed to her, under the circumstances, pathetic. She tried to recall the last fleeting memories from the night before. She could not remember faces. She had flashes of hairy men, like animals, with bad smells mounting her, turning her over, tearing her apart, their laughter and grunting accentuated by her screams. She recalled that all the men had beards that scratched her. Where was Juan? He had no beard. Why didn't he save her?

She turned to Juan with a dazed look showing a mix between perplexity and disgust and asked in crude Castellano, "Where you?"

Juan tried to explain with an empty olive jar that he drank too much and went into a deep sleep. Juan was relieved to understand that Avante did not consider him as one of her rapists. In Avante's mind, she recalled that it was Juan who brought the jar of spirits to the meeting place, and although he did not participate, he was not strong enough to save her. She realized that she could not count on Juan for any strength of any kind.

'I must count on myself. What is happening to me? Breathe deep. What is my situation? I am hurt, and the 'nokfilaki' have violated me. Get up! Walk! Yes, you can leave here. Where to? I am carrying the spend of those creatures in me. I must get it out. Don't go to the creek and be seen. Walk to the river to the east.'

Avante put on her clothes and, without a word to Juan, set out toward the sunrise. Juan began to follow and she screamed at him "No! Go back!"

He turned and left. Avante proceeded to the small river, recently christened "San Juan" and washed herself out. Now, she thought, the hard part. She returned to her house and there, as expected, she found her mother and father waiting for her, as well as Ayo, who had come from his wife's home. All Avante's bruises were on her private parts. There were no marks of struggle on her face.

Therefore, Avante, obviously guilty of something, decided to confess to the lesser of all crimes. "Yes. I slipped out of the house when you were sleeping and met with Juan, a soldier at the barracks. We went to sleep and woke up at dawn. Nothing happened!"

Her parents took this information and said they would get back with her in the evening about a punishment.

Avante then left for Xequina's house to accompany her down the trail to Joara and from there to prepare the soldier's breakfast. Avante confided everything to Xequina with the purpose of seeking advice to avoid pregnancy. Vara was there at the open kitchen in the soldier's plaza. When Xequina told Vara about what had happened to Avante, Vara immediately left work and went off into the forest to find the fresh plants she needed for a concoction.

Juan Sanchez did not appear for breakfast, but he was at the soldier's mess table for the late lunch. Avante served him his food as if nothing had happened. He stayed eating after his comrades had left. Avante sat down beside him and asked, "Who are the men?"

Juan replied, "They are watching us now. Meet me when the five bells ring at the place where women wash clothes." He made sure Avante understood this, then they departed.

Late that afternoon at five bells, Juan met Avante at the washing place, the same place where, the previous year, Vara had been attacked and saved by Juancinto. They waded up-steam in the creek about 250 yards until they came to a place where the creek was within shouting distance of Barracks Number One and the Spanish Plaza. From their hiding place below the bank of the creek they could see the plaza. Juan was able to point out to Avante which of the men was Domingo Calera and the other two men involved in the crime, Luis de Mendana, and Alvaro de Aguilar.

Late that evening, Juan Lopez Sanchez left Barracks Number One to relieve himself by the creek not far from the place where he had, earlier that afternoon, hid with Avante. He did not return to the barracks that night.

At dawn, when the door to Barracks Number One was opened, there lying on the ground in front of the door was a ball-game racket. Stuffed in the netting of the racket was a hairy black object. One soldier picked up the racket and emptied out the contents onto the ground. It was the scalp of Juan Sanchez, identified by his long black hair. Bound within the bloody scalp, as if packaged like a gift, were the penis and testicles of the youth.

All were aghast and horrified. Some turned away and retched. Domingo Calera, Luis de Mendana, and Alvaro de Aguilar were terrified.

The news flashed around Joara like a lightning bolt. A runner met Avante and Xequina along the creek path as they were going to the kitchen to work. When the runner mentioned the ball game racket and the scalp with long black hair Avante knew instantly what had happened. She had seen the calamity unfold in her dream the previous morning as Juan whispered in her ear to wake up. Ayo had taken matters into his own hands and quietly murdered and mutilated him. This realization was quickly followed by the implication that she was just as responsible for Juan's innocent death as Ayo.

Why hadn't she told the truth that she had been raped by three soldiers, or better, why had she not kept her mouth shut, letting her parents believe that she wandered off without an explanation? Now she knew that if she were to identify Domingo and the others there would be an actual war. Ayo and his friends would avenge the crime in the same way, and the Spaniards would not stand for it.

When Avante reached her house, she asked her mother if she had seen Ayo. "No," was the reply.

Then Avante stormed back down the path to Joara and over to the neighborhood where Ayo stayed with his new wife. Avante asked about the whereabouts of Ayo and was told that Ayo had left the previous night, telling his wife that he would not be back until the Spaniards were gone. By the Spanish calendar, it was the second week in April 1568.

CHAPTER 14

CONFLAGRATION

CREEK, CHEROKEE AND CATAWBA
TERRITORIES
LATE APRIL 1568

What would have taken a normal man to do in three days, Ayo did in two, in part due to the physical stamina he achieved as captain of the ball team, and in part due to the urgency he sensed in the air. He was not running from Spanish justice; on the contrary, his blood boiled with anticipation that the time of his people's retribution had arrived, and he was being called by the Great Spirit to carry out Joaran justice on the Spanish. He knew he was not alone. Great forces were gathering on the mountain.

At the end of the first day he reached the mountain, and by following the Swannanoa River he ascended to the ridge through Joara Gap. By nightfall of the second day, he had reached the French Broad River with endless campfires lineding both banks of the river at the village of Tocae. Earlier in the afternoon, he began to encounter various small parties fishing and hunting for game. They were, for the most part, Cherokee, and Creek from as far away as Coosa. They told Ayo of the great powwow assembled at Tocae. The revolt had begun six days ago in Chiaha. Now the Spanish forts in Olamico and Cauchi were destroyed, and the tribes were gathering in Tocae before descending on to Joara. Ayo sensed that, with the guidance of the Great Spirit, his own timing was impeccable.

Ayo entered Tocae looking for the lodgings of the war chiefs. He was met with much noise and celebration, some of which were unconstrained due to the communal wine taken from the storehouses in Olamico and

Cauchi. By his dress, he was recognized as Catawban, and was even asked if he was the one called Ayo. Apparently, his reputation as a ballplayer and a future war chief had preceded him even up into these mountains. Ayo was directed to the house where Gueza, the great War Chief of Coosa, was staying. There he was warmly greeted by Gueza and the War Chiefs of Olamico, Cauchi, and Tocae.

The arrival of Ayo struck them as providential because they were just in the process of planning the attack on the Spanish Fort at Joara. Ayo informed them that he killed a soldier from the fort in Joara three nights ago, and he knew that the morale of the soldiers there was bad and that there were only 39 of them. These war chiefs were curious and glad to hear this because, with a fort and three barracks, they were assuming that Joara had over 100 Spanish soldiers. The confirmation of their overestimation of the power of the Spaniards was good news.

Ayo told the war chiefs that he had practically run from Joara non-stop and that he was anxious to discuss a war plan, but he wished to bathe, eat, and get some rest first, so perhaps the next morning would be better. They agree and a sent word to have a nearby lodging prepared for Ayo.

"In the meantime," Ayo suggested, "could the great war chiefs inform me about how the fighting went in Olamico and Cauchi?"

The elderly warriors laughed, "It was not much of a fight, in either case."

The Olamico War Chief remarked, "At the Spanish stockade in Olamico we lost about 30 braves to their crossbows and harquebuses. We ended up with only 20 of their scalps. Five of their soldiers drowned and floated down the river before we could take the time to scalp them."

There was some laughter.

"When did it happen?" Ayo asked.

Gueza related, "It was six days ago. Our main force of 300 warriors swam to the south tip of the long island. It was close to dawn. We proceeded north along the island with all the women, children, and old men behind us. There was no resistance until we got to within a crossbow's shot of the palisades. While this was happening, two other forces of 150 warriors, our best archers, each positioned themselves on the opposite shores at the northern tip of the island, where the river splits into two channels. Do you know that the Spanish fort was next to our

Council Mound at the northern tip of the island? We anticipated that the soldiers would try to escape to the north, and this was the case. We mounted the palisade wall from the south with ladders, and once inside, opened the gate.

"This is where we lost our men due to the Spanish fire sticks and lead arrows. In a very short time we covered the Spanish fort with flaming arrows. From the top of our Sacred Mound we fired into the little fort and killed many before they escaped toward the northern palisade wall. Our archers picked them off the wall as they climbed it. Those that got overe the wall jumped into the river at the tip of the island. Those that could not swim drowned in the river. Most of the others were shot in the water by our best bowmen. Those who made it to the bank of the river were met with tomahawks and war hammers. There were no survivors."

"And Cauchi?" Ayo asked, "What happened there?"

Gueza continued, "The Spanish fort there was destroyed easier and quicker than the one at Olamico—fire arrows from hills above. There was no escape for the soldiers at Cauchi; all were scalped, but for one."

"And what happened to him?" Ayo asked.

"Believe it or not," the Olamico War Chief stated, "that big *nofilacki* was the one who is married to the daughter our Orata at Olamico. Her name is Immokalee, and she is a wild one. She and her husband were warned and allowed to escape from Cauchi downriver to Canosagua, where there was another *nokfilaki,* who is married to the daughter of the medicine man there."

Just then a boy stuck his head through the door to announce that the lodging was ready for the warrior from Joara.

Ayo thanked the War Chiefs for their update and begged forgiveness for being so tired but he would be much fresher first thing in the morning. He then departed.

The next morning Ayo met with the War Chiefs and it was determined that they would attack Joara on the night of the next full moon, which was three nights from that morning. They determined they had about 1000 warriors, to be divided up between Ayo, Gueza and the War Chiefs from Olamico and Cauchi. At about midnight, each war party would approach Joara from one of the four cardinal points and surprise the soldiers in their sleep, encircling the Spanish Plaza, preventing anyone from escaping.

This determined, the vast assemblage of warriors gathered their gear and set out on the trail east toward the Joara Gap. At twilight, they had made camp on an Eastern Ridge of Black Mountain, overlooking miles of rolling green plain. Far below, the twisting gap trail was disappearing in the fading light, while the sight of cook fires sprang up from the settlements along the Swannanoa headwaters to the south and the Catawba headwaters to the north.

Ayo sent out a messenger to run through the night and next day to deliver a message to Joara Mico. The message stated that a large party of Creek and Cherokee warriors would begin their attack the night of the full moon, in two nights. He should keep this as a secret unto himself until the night of the attack as warriors begin coming through the neighborhoods approaching the Spanish fort. At the first sign of this, Joara Mico should send out the order for all Joaran warriors to join their brothers from the mountains in the destruction of the Spanish fort.

Early the next morning, the vast war party descended the mountain and, following the Catawba River, made camp in the forests surrounding the great meadow where the ball game against Guatari had been played six months earlier. Ayo was not worried that the war party might be discovered because he knew, per agreement, that all the hunting was done by Joaran hunters. The Spanish soldiers now kept to the confines of the fort, and especially so now that a killer was loose.

That night, Ayo took a canoe and paddled by down the river to Warrior Creek. From there, he went on foot overland without being seen or attracting attention, skirting around the town to the house of his parents in the hills to the north. He woke them up, as well as his sister. He told Avante that for the sake of herself, the family, the clan, and the town, he had to avenge her violation and desecration. She informed him that he had killed the wrong Spaniard. "Juan did not rape me!"

Ayo expressed his sorrow at this, but offered, "If it were any consolation, I killed your Juan outright. He did not suffer the mutilation of his body. However, that will not be the case for the other three."

Ayo went to the nearby house of Xequina, knowing where she slept, and knocked on the wall where he thought her head would be. Sure enough, she awoke and proceeded to sneak out of the house, expecting to find Ruy. To her shock, it was Ayo, who put his hand over her mouth to stop her from shouting. Ayo whispered to Xequina, "You must leave Joara tomorrow with your Spaniard if you want to have a life with him. Tomorrow night the fort will be attacked by warriors from the mountains and no one will be left alive. Do you hear?"

"Yes, Ayo, I hear. I will do as you say. Can I tell Vara and her man, Davide, to come with us? The four of us can survive better than two."

"Yes, Vara and her man can go with you and I can tell you now, Xequina, that there is news that two more of the *nokfilaki*, perhaps friends of your men escaped the destruction of Cauchi probably because both have married Indian women. They are staying with their wives in Canosaqui, the location of those famous hot springs downriver from Cauchi. The bad news is that it would be too dangerous for you to go there. After tomorrow night, all Spaniards are supposed to be dead. If your men are discovered alive on the plain or within the mountains it could be dangerous for them."

"Where should we go then, Ayo?"

Ayo responded, "I suggest that it would be best to go toward Table Rock where the sun now sets in the west. You know the little river there which comes out of the great Gorge. If you leave tomorrow night and travel by the light of the moon you will be there by daylight. But be careful, Xequina. You dare not go too far up into the Gorge."

"Why do you say that Ayo? Why should we not dare to go as far as we can?" asked Xequina.

Ayo answered, "The Gorge has always been a no-man's land. It is a wild place, a territory reserved for outlaws, outcasts, and misfits. There are many ways to die up there: becoming lost, falling from the rocks, disturbing animals or men. But for now, by that same token, the Gorge, at least the mouth of the Gorge, will be a safe refuge for you both and your men. No one will venture into the Gorge looking for Spaniards, but if you want to be sure, about two leagues up into the Gorge on the west slope there is a cave you could stay in."

"Ayo," Xequina stated with tears in her eyes, "I am so grateful for your warning and advice. You, indeed, are a great man, but may I ask you why you are doing this kind act?"

Ayo paused for a moment and stated, "I have seen that the Spaniards are men like ourselves; a few are good, and a few are evil and the rest somewhere in between but inclined to follow what is more powerful. I took the law into my own hands and killed Avante's Juan, and I am bound to undertake more killing tomorrow night. With all this killing I do not want to destroy any remnant of good inside myself. Today my heart caused me to think of you and your man, Ruy, and how good he was for Joara on the ball field. With so much evil, I wanted to do something to balance on the side of good, for myself, the town, and for you and the one you love."

That night Ayo returned over the fields to the great meadow and the surrounding forests where the war camps of over a thousand warriors were assembled. The next day final preparations were made and, by nightfall, the movement of men to surround Joara had begun.

Gueza, the paramount Commander, led 250 men on the approach to Joara from the west. They left the Catawba Meadows and crossed the river, proceeding east toward Joara at a swift pace. Close to midnight they had entered the little valley at the eastern end of which lay Joara. They crept through clan neighborhoods and across fields and gardens until they were within sight of the Sacred Mound, the fort, and the four buildings beside it. As they proceeded, they were reinforced by local warriors from the neighborhoods.

From the south, the war chief from Olamico led a party of warriors in canoes down the Catawba River to where Warrior Creek flowed into it on the left side. This party of 350 fighters walked up Warrior Creek, alerting five villages of the imminent attack on the Spanish fort and mustered additional help.

A third war party led by Tocae's War Chief took 40 canoes down the Catawba past the juncture with Warrior Creek and down to where the San Juan River joins the Catawba on the north side. They traveled in canoes up the San Juan River to a point opposite the town of Joara, a mile or so to the west. From there, they disembarked and approached Joara from the east, alerting the villagers along the way.

Ayo led the fourth war party of about 150 warriors. They departed from Catawba Meadows and proceeded over land and into the hills north of the Joara valley and into the neighborhood where Ayo grew up. Xequina, Ruy, Vara and Davide had left from the same neighborhood two hours prior, heading in the direction of Table Rock. Xequina guided the foursome silently west in the moonlight. She was familiar with the trail and expected that Ayo and his warriors might be on it. She hid in the brush with the other three when she spotted dark movement in the moonlight on the hills ahead. From their hiding place, they watched the war party pass, all bare-chested and painted, glistening in the moonlight, moving swiftly to the sound and rhythm of moccasins hitting the clay path.

Toward midnight all four war parties had reached their positions surrounding Joara. No Spaniard had yet been alerted, and the stirred-up villagers that were amassing behind the warriors were mum with eager expectation.

Four sentries were guarding the three barracks of the fort, but their minds were not on their surroundings. All others were inside playing card games or asleep with their dreams.

From the direction of the northern neighborhoods came the sound of three owl hoots. Then, moments later, the sound was duplicated from the east, followed by the south, and then the west. When Ayo heard the three hoots coming from the west, he began the attack. The men moved swiftly down the path beside Warrior Creek until they advanced to the fishing bench where Avante and Juan used to meet. There they laid down the kettles of boiling pine resin they had been carrying. Hundreds of arrows were dipped into the brew, soaking the leather that was wrapped around the shaft up to the tip.

This done, they continued down the path to within sight of the two northern barracks. From a common torch all the arrows were lit. Ayo asserted his right for the first shot. He launched a flaming arrow high in the air, and it landed on the wood shake roof of one of the new barrack structures. Then, suddenly, dozens of flaming arrows showered down upon the three barracks roofs. The sight of these flames was the sign for the other war parties to move forward, tightening the noose around the fort and preventing any soldiers from escaping.

A bugle was sounded, but the alert was interrupted by an arrow in the chest of the bugler. Ten soldiers in the first barracks crowded through the doorway. Most were killed near the entrance, but a few got away running south across the plaza and into the fort defended by the dry moat and palisade wall.

What happened at the first barrack happened in a similar measure at the other two barracks. During the course of 20 minutes, all three structures were aflame and 20 of the 39 soldiers of the garrison, who half an hour previously were playing cards or dreaming, now lay in the soil of the Spanish plaza, some dead and some alive, as their scalps were cut away from their skulls. With the barracks decimated, the other three war parties approached the walled stockade, from east, south, and west. Ayo climbed the Sacred Mound and shot the first flaming arrow down onto the wooden roof, less than 100 feet away. Within a minute, the two-story structure was covered with burning arrows. The remaining 19 soldiers were in a panic, knowing 200 pounds of harquebuse powder was about to explode. They fled through the palisade gate and jumped into the dry moat. They were all half-naked, some with swords, running around in the moat like rats. As they tried to climb out, dozens of Indians would laughingly push them back into the moat. They were enjoying the scene too much to kill them.

Then an explosion occurred with such sound and devastation that no one on either side of the Ocean Sea had ever before experienced. The storehouse was blasted apart, leaving a crater the size of a pond, and most of the palisade wall had collapsed on top of the hapless Spanish soldiers in the moat. All but 8 soldiers were now buried, blown apart or scalped. These 8 were now crouched in the moat beside the remaining palisade wall crying like babies and begging for mercy.

Erbani, standing on the edge of the moat, looked closely at the 8, and recognized that 3 were the ones that Juan Sanchez, before he disappeared, had identified to Avante on the day after the rape. He could not believe his eyes. These three survived the explosion. '*What is the Great Spirit saying?*', he asked himself. He even knew their names as Vara had passed this information to him. They were Domingo Calera, Luis de Mendana and Alvaro de Aquilar.

Ayo witnessed the destruction of the fort from atop the Sacred Mound. Erbani saw him and ran up the steps to convey to Ayo that the three rapists were still alive in the moat. Ayo descended the mound and made his way into the moat. Erbani followed him. Walking through the debris, Ayo stumbled upon the dead body of Villamar, the ensign and commanding officer. He picked up Villamar's sword and, pulling Erbani with him, made his way to the 8 survivors, huddled together amid the wreckage. He gave 5 of the 8 Spainards to the warriors who were following him with instructions to do with them what they wanted.

Alvaro de Aguilar was clutching a gold crucifix which he wore on a chain around his neck. Ayo approached him and, grabbing the crucifix, pulled Alvaro up into a standing position. Then he yanked the crucifix off his neck. Ayo examined it closely. It was the kind that had the limp body of Jesus Christ hung from the cross. He glanced over at Erbani and said, "Translate this."

Ayo looked at the three whimpering souls, huddled together, and held up the crucifix in their faces, asking, "Is this how you think you should die, to redeem yourself for the violation of my sister? There is enough wood here. We can arrange it very quickly. No. In my mercy, I will give you another choice. On the one hand, I will build for each of you a cross and bind you to it. Then I will make a small fire at the base and watch you roast slowly, or, you can kneel here and tell me what you are going to say to Jesus Christ, your Savior, about your crime, to convince him to let you into the spirit world."

All three chose the second option and knelt on all four's in the moat, looking up at Ayo. Sword in hand, Ayo stood above Alvaro and asked him to introduce himself to Jesus Christ and explain why he should be allowed into heaven after raping a 15-year-old girl.

"I am Alvaro de Aguilar. I was born in Salamanca. My family was poor but very religious, especially my dear mother, who is praying for me now. Because of her, I was taught the catechism. There was no work in Salamanca for me, so I joined the army and wound up here. I was told we were here to convert the heathens to Christianity. The truth is, I did not feel that I belonged in this place. I am not strong. I have never been strong, and I have always sought the protection of people stronger than myself. I felt protected and safe by being a member of Domingo's gang. So, when he ordered us to get the girl drunk and rape her, we did it without asking any questions. I am weak, and I am ashamed of myself."

With this statement, Ayo, after hearing the translation, brought the sword down upon Alvaro's thin neck with all the strength he could muster, saying, "May the Great Spirit have mercy on your weak soul." The head rolled to the ground, followed by a torrent of blood.

Ayo next turned to Luis. "Your story?"

"I am Luis de Mendana. My home is Toledo, but I never really had a home. My parents died or gave me away to the Church when I was five.

No one ever told me the truth. I was raised in an orphanage by friars. One friar took advantage of me for years and led me to believe that that kind of sex-act was permitted and approved in the sight of God."

Ayo did not want to hear any more explanation. He said, "I will put you out of your misery," and brought the sword down upon the neck of Luis de Mendana. Because his neck was thicker than Alvaro's and the sword was duller, and perhaps because Ayo was tiring, it took three chops with a fresh hatchet for Ayo to separate Luis's head from his body.

Ayo then turned to Domingo, "Now you, you are the oldest and the mastermind behind this crime. You led these boys into the evil world. Who are you, and what is your excuse? What are you going to say to your Savior?"

"I am Domino Calera. I am from Malaga, and I have no Savior. Without evil, the good could not be recognized or even exist; therefore, being evil, I make possible the good. That is what I would tell Jesus! I will also say that your sister enjoyed the wine until she passed out with Juan, her protector. Yes, your sister had a beautiful body," he snarled, "and I enjoyed it." Domingo was expecting these to be his last words, but Ayo had other ideas.

"And did you see her naked?"

"Of course."

Ayo then had a few of the witnessing warriors hold the man down, while, with the sword, he gouged out one eye from the head of the howling man.

"I have left one eye for you to see what is going to happen next. I will not even ask if you penetrated her."

Ayo ordered the men to remove Domingo's pants. Picking up a piece of a palisade pole, still burning at one end, Ayo ordered the warriors to spread his legs apart and make him straddle the pole with the hot embers against his testicles and penis. Domingo was screaming uncontrollably and begging Ayo for mercy. Ayo said, "I will give you mercy after you watch this with your one good eye." He had Domingo's male organ stretched out on the smoldering log and, with the sword, began chopping it off inch by inch, until Domingo fainted and fell off the log.

At this point, Ayo gave the sword to a nearby warrior, saying, "I've had enough. Take his body parts home for trophies if you want."

Ayo left the fiery fort and retired to the house of his wife in the Paint Clan neighborhood. He slept until dawn and was ready to begin the trip downriver to Guatarí and Canos, hoping to get there before the arrival of the news of the burning of Fort San Juan. But the mood in Joara was jubilant, and all the warriors were tired. It was decided between the Mico Joara and Mico Coosa just to celebrate and enjoy the day. The next day the Creek and Cherokee warriors began heading back into the mountains, leaving the destruction of forts at Canos and Guatari to their Catawban brothers under the command of Ayo, now the undisputed War Chief of Joara.

After a day of celebration, Ayo set about commandeering 80 canoes from the villages along Warrior Creek and San Juan River. Assembling on the Catawba, 300 warriors from this area they began the trip downstream, reaching the first stage, the village of Quinahaqui, in a day and a half. There they stored their canoes and continued overland for another two days to reach the Chiefdom to Guatari on the Yadkin River. The garrison of 19 men at Fort Santiago was alerted to the approach of the Joaran War Party and put up resistance in their larger fort and chapel. The Joaran warriors lost ten men due to crossbow and harquebuse fire, but within two hours, the Spanish structures were engulfed in flame, and the surviving soldiers put to death.

The priest, Sebastian Montero, was at that time in Santa Elena. He had generated a following and had the trust of the women Micos of Guatari. Maybe, for this reason, the warriors of Guatari offered little help to those of Joara in cleansing their Chiefdom of the Spanish invaders. All of Guatarí recognized Ayo, the War Chief, as the captain of the ball team that had defeated them.

After Guatarí, the war party retraced its route back to the Catawba River and paddled south with the current for five days before reaching the old Chiefdom of Canos. They arrived in the last days of that violent month of April 1568. The newly built Fort Tomas in Canos had recently been occupied six weeks prior by 30 soldiers sent there by Juan Pardo to mitigate the food shortage at Santa Elena. The soldiers had no warning as they watched, in wonder, 80 canoes pull up at the bank of the river, and discharged hundreds of warriors. Some ran for the sanctuary of the fort, others surrendered outright, and a few fought valiantly, though in vain.

For those Spanish souls of Fort San Tomas who surrendered Ayo gave the same the opportunity to stand before their Savior and explain themselves. With the death of the last Spaniard, Ayo vowed never again to hear the chatter of Spanish soldiers reverberate along the rivers of the land.

By the time the great war party paddled back up to Joara, plans were well underway to enlarge the Sacred Mound with the debris from the Spanish occupation. The mound doubled in size and served the native people for more than a century thereafter as a symbol of the power of Joara to preserve the traditional way from the advance of the Sea-Foam People.

***

It is true that in subsequent times, those rivers, those "Long Men" of the Divine Earth from the Tennessee River to the Catawba River, would rarely again hear the sharpm tongue of Spain.

But the after effects of the *nokfilaki,* the Sea-Foam People, were insidious, despite the scarcity of their physical presence. Within a generation of Ayo, smallpox began to flood the land, rendering, for some unknown reason, the Catawba people more susceptible to its devastation than most other tribal nations. As if that plague were not enough, the Catawba were particularly susceptible to the poison of alcohol and firearms, in the form of trade goods flowing down the trade path from Richmond and up the path from Charleston. Thus smallpox, alcohol, greed, and a general loss of wisdom forced the Catawba Nation to shrink into a few protected villages along the Catawba River about halfway between the legendary Chiefdoms of Joara and Canos. But this is another story.

CHAPTER 15

JUANCINTO'S LAST MISSION

CANOSAQUI – APRIL-MAY 1568-SANTA ELENA – JUNE 1568-1576

After the destruction of Fort San Juan, Coosa Mico and Olamico Orata stopped in Canosaqui on their return to Creek territory. Olamico Orata was anxious to spend a day or two with his daughter, Immokalee, who was now living there with her *nokfilaki* husband, Daniel Almeyda. Coosa Mico had heard of the adventure of Immokalee with her husband and his friend at the Big Suck. Now he was looking forward to meeting them, especially the friend, Juan Martín, who was now married to Quhana, the daughter of Suye'ti, the famous medicine man of Canosaqui.

To Coosa Mico, this Daniel and Juan were apparently two anomalies that defied the profile of the typical Spanish *nokfilaki*, a profile that had festered the past 26 years. He wanted to meet these two aberrations of *nokfilaki* nature and learn something that perhaps he could use for his final blow against the Spanish intruders.

Coosa Mico enjoyed the day of festivities and relaxed in the thermal waters with Olamico Orata, Suye'ti, their daughters and their husbands. At the end of the day, Coosa Mico was confirmed in his intuition, Juan Martín de Badajoz was the man for the task he had in mind.

He confronted Juan and Quhana, face to face in the bubbling waters. "I want you to do something very important for the future of the Cherokee, Creek, and Catawba people."

"What is it, Coosa Mico?" Juancinto responded.

"I want you to go to Santa Elena, leaving tomorrow, as the sole survivor of the destruction of all five forts."

Juancinto paused for a few moments and then had Quhana help him with the translation. He ventured, "Coosa Mico, I know of only three forts that have been destroyed."

The Paramount Chief responded, "By the time you get to Santa Elena, all five forts will be destroyed. You are to tell your Captain Pardo that you were stationed at Joara with the other 39 men, and on the night of the attack you had gone into the bushes to relieve yourself. From there, you watched the catastrophe, and you didn't know what to do but to follow the river and trails down to Santa Elena."

"But Coosa Mico," Juancinto responded, "Captain Pardo knows, and the records show that I was stationed at Cauchi."

"Then you can tell him that you watched the fort in Cauchi destroyed, and then traveled down the river passed Joara, where you overheard that it was destroyed, as well as, the forts in Guatarí and Canos. Or you can tell him that you were repositioned down to Joara. It does not matter. You are to appear before Captain Pardo and his superiors as the only survivor from all five forts. That is the only message."

"Yes, I can do this, Coosa Mico, however, you know I am married to Quhana, and she is with child. I am sure that if I go to Santa Elena they will not let me come back."

"Yes, I understand, but you cannot go with Quhana. We will send her down to Santa Elena after two moons. She will say she is pregnant and you are the father. You will confirm this and be with her."

"But she cannot travel alone, and I will have trouble myself passing through all those lands," Juancinto responded.

"Yes, therefore, you will be in a long canoe with an escort of three warriors. They will take you as far as Guiomae, and from there you will travel overland to Orista. From Orista, you will be taken in a canoe to Santa Elena. After two moons, we will do the same for Quhana."

"Very well, Coosa Mico," Juancinto answered, "I will have to talk it over with Quhana to see if she agrees."

"No, Juan, there is nothing to talk over. We have to do this," Quhana asserted.

"Very well, then. When do I leave?" Juancinto asked.

"Tomorrow at sunrise," Coosa Mico answered.

"Why so soon?"

"Because I want you to deliver the bad news before Captain Pardo and his men come again into our land. I want them to see and be convinced that just as 26 years ago when Hernando de Soto's invasion of our land ended in failure, so this last invasion has ended in even greater devastation. That means to say that the Spaniards are no match for the project. Tell them to save their lives and wealth, and don't come back!"

The next day was April 23, 1568 and the plan was set in motion. Juan Martín de Badajóz arrived in Santa Elena two weeks later. On the way down the Catawba River at the village of Quinahaqui, Juancinto took note of the fact that about 80 canoes had been pulled up onto the shore, confirming to Juancinto that Guatarí was surely meeting the same fate as Joara. Four days later, when Juancinto sped past the major town in the Chiefdom of Canos, Juancinto had to hide in the canoe, as he could see that Fort San Tomás was still standing, and the garrison was enjoying a lazy spring afternoon. The news from the north had not yet reached Canos, and this news would be delivered to Fort San Tomás by Ayo and his war party in short order.

A week later, Juan Martín arrived by foot at the village of Orista in the territorial jurisdiction of Santa Elena. Juan Martín asked Orista Orata about his son-in-law Rufín. He was told that Rufín was still in Santa Elena, as far as the Orata knew, and he had not visited for a long time. Juan Martín was supplied with a canoe and a young man to paddle him over to Santa Elena. This gave him some quiet time to conserve his energy and think about how he was going to present the bad news.

Juancinto imagined standing in a room with only Captain Pardo and Adelantado Pedro Menéndez. He would tell them that all the forts were destroyed and that, as far as he knew, he was the only survivor. That was all there was to tell, except how he had escaped because he was relieving himself in the bushes. He tried to imagine how their faces would change and even distort with the news that all their plans and efforts for the past two years had come to nothing but death and destruction. He would be a simple messenger who had traveled overland for two weeks to deliver this important message.

He could not predict if the Gypsy soul, Juancinto Taranto, would secretly celebrate in the scene he imagined delivering. The tragic news would be over-whelming to these two men of great influence in the "*gajo*" world of the Spanish Empire, and those around them would hear them cry and gnash their teeth in anger and frustration. Juancinto's whole life had been under the thumb, or at least, the structure of the rules of the Royal Family of Castile and Aragon, as well as the Holy Roman Church. He had either played by these rules or worked around them. For Juancinto Taranto, now it was strangely disconcerting that he, a Gypsy from Seville, was the bearer of the news of this import—that the latest attempts to establish the Spanish Order in this vast part of the New World had come to nothing. He resolved that when delivering the news, he would *not* secretly revel in it, but wear his Spanish Soul and feel the gravity of the circumstance.

Then there was also Juancinto Taranto, the wanderer, and outlaw. Reflecting on his current circumstances, Juancinto realized that his life, unlike his Spanish compatriots, was more like the experience of his Portuguese Jewish blood-brothers, his brothers in crime, always on the outside, always on the run. Yes, his Gypsy-self, his blood-brother-self, would celebrate in a deep and hidden Gypsy way, the delivery of the terrible news, so devastating to the prospect of the non-Gypsy world of Spain in La Florida.

But now he was aware of a third Juancinto. One that first appeared in Colombia and grew or matured in some strange way with each broken heart. This was the Juancinto who had been taught noble compassion, generosity, and love by Atora, the wise daughter of the Muisca High Priest. She had now forgiven him of his weakness for gold. This was the Juancinto who was taught to read music and words by Nani, all for the purpose of healing others. This was the Juancinto who was saved and was reborn on the canal bridge in Seville by his mother-in-law, La Gitanilla, who told him he must live because he had more to do in life. Now he was married to Quhana, who was the equal of this third Juancinto. She brought his life together. She brought his world home. She was his wife, now bearing his first child since Quim. What did this mean to his soul? Was his soul Spanish, Gypsy, or Cherokee? He must go with his heart. His soul would now be Indian; it would be Cherokee.

His Cherokee soul had been given a mission; to deliver such devastating news that it would discourage any more Spanish encroachment into the lands of the Cherokee, Creek, and Catawba—forever.

And so, Juan Martín de Badajoz delivered the news to Adelantado Menéndez and Captain Juan Pardo just as Coosa Mico had instructed him. He made up all the gruesome details his imagination could conjure up. It was the saddest of all days at Fort San Felipe of Santa Elena, which had already experienced many sad days and would experience many more.

Within two months, Quhana arrived at Santa Elena, thus fulfilling the promise by Coosa Mico. Juan had to admit to his comrades and superiors that he was, indeed, married, and his pregnant new wife had followed him, through the force of love, to Santa Elena.

Juan and Quhana were formally married in the chapel at Santa Elena, and she changed her name to Teresa Martín de Badajoz. Soon thereafter, their first child was born. She was christened and recorded in the registry as Ines, but her secret name was "Atora." The birth of Inez was soon followed by the birth of a sister named on the books for her mother Teresa, but at home they called her "Nani."

It was soon evident to the community of farm families, soldiers, and elite administrators at Santa Elena that Teresa Martín was no ordinary Indian woman. Besides being an excellent translator, she was adept at gathering, not only herbal medicines, but various nuts, berries, and roots that would help sustain Santa Elena through poor crop harvests due to drought, flood, and just plain unproductive soil.

What Juancinto had not fully considered, and perhaps it was the fault of his Gypsy-self, was that on returning to Santa Elena he would be returning to the circumstances of his short professional life as a soldier under the flag of the Houses of Castile and Aragon. That meant, of course, that he would continue to be paid and perform the duties of a soldier in the army of the King. Perhaps, as a concept, this was not so bad, but what Juancinto had not foreseen was that his commanding officer would once again be Sergeant Moyano. Yes, the very Sergeant Moyano who had escaped annihilation by accompanying Captain Pardo and his expedition back to Santa Elena. Moyano had only done so after convincing Juan Pardo to make a special stop, for about a week, near the town of Yssa on the fork of Catawba River where Moyano showed Pardo the crystal mountain he had previously discovered along with the prospective mines in the area.

Now Juan Martín de Badajoz would have to be in daily contact with Sergeant Moyano. On the one hand, this was not so bad because Sergeant

Moyano admired Juan for many reasons: his skill with a razor, his fearlessness, and most of all for his ability to have experienced all the things Moyano had lived through in the wild interior and still found a way, like himself, to make it back to civilization. For Moyano, only one other person had lived this experience to the extent Juan Martín had, and that person was himself. Being held in such esteem by his commanding officer, Juan received special treatment. In short, Moyano felt that he and Juan Martín were members of an exclusive brotherhood.

Juancinto did not see it like this. He saw Sergeant Moyano as embodying all the characteristics of the Spanish personality that he despised. He could even imagine Moyano making a pass at Solea while she danced in a public square, and he could see himself slitting Moyano's throat. Juancinto hated Moyano with all three of his souls: Spanish, Gypsy, and Cherokee. Yet, for five full years, Juan Martín de Badajoz played the game as Sergeant Moyano's favorite.

Both Juancinto and Quhana reasoned that now, with a family which included two little girls, the distance between this god-forsaken island and their beloved Cherokee Mountains had grown considerably. There was no certainty that a half *nokfilaki* family could walk over 350 miles in hostile terrain, and even if they could, on Juan's still meager wages, they could not save up enough to buy the axe-heads, chisels, knives, and glass beads that would grease their way through the difficult passage. They would wait for the girls to grow for the right opportunity to return home.

Since the massacres at the interior forts living conditions for the 300 unhappy souls of this "capital" of La Florida had deteriorated with each passing year. Juancinto and Quhana speculated that maybe things in Santa Elena would get so bad that there would be a revolt among the Indians. Santa Elena would disappear, and then they could go back to the mountains.

Soon after the destruction of the forts, Captain Pardo left for other parts. Adelantado Menéndez stayed sailing between Santa Elena and San Augustin and made several trips to Spain and back, and finally dying in 1574, after being accused in the Spanish court of failing to provide the colonists with the promised cattle, and keeping all the colonists on the seacoast, "which is all sand and not fruitful." During these years, a series of men were appointed to be Governors of Santa Elena each surpassing the other in appropriating for themselves treasury funds and supplies and other people's property and wives. This was done with almost no regard for peaceful relations with the Indian villages on the banks of the rivers surrounding Santa Elena.

By the summer of 1576, eight years after the massacres at the forts, the Indian rebellion that Juancinto and Quhana were expecting, arrived.

Alonso Solis had just been appointed as the new Governor of Santa Elena and had learned nothing from his predecessors. He tyrannized and abused the Indians. For no clear reason, he killed a chief named Humalo, who, years previously, had accompanied Adelantado Menéndez to Spain and returned to foster good-will. Solis then hung another Indian leader at Santa Elena and killed a chieftain of the Guale Tribe, further down the coast. The Indians from Guale and Orista, although of different nations, were close neighbors. They rose up together in rebellion.

On 17th of June in 1576, Sergeant Hernando Moyano was promoted to Ensign. Shortly thereafter in response to the perpetual lack of food in Santa Elena, Hernando Moyano and 21 soldiers under his command, were sent by orders from the Fort at Santa Elena to go upriver to the Indian village of Escamacu, sister village to the nearby Orista, to forage for food among the Indians. When they arrived the villagers were celebrating a festival. Ensign Moyano and men appeared, demanding food. The Indians told Moyano they had no extra food. Moyano did not believe them and threatened them with his sword. The Indians fled into the nearby woods. Corporal Juan Martín de Badajoz advised Moyano that it was too dangerous to stay any longer where they were. Ensign Moyano laughed at this advice then ordered his soldiers to light the fuses of their harquebuses in case of attack. The old chief of Escamacu came out of the woods to talk with Moyano. He asked why Moyano wanted to start a war? Moyano replied that he had no wish to make war; instead, he was just looking for a place to spend the night and food to take back to the garrison at Fort San Felipe.

To this, the chief replied, "Why then did the soldiers keep their fuses lit if they intended no harm?" The chief assured Moyano that if the soldiers would extinguish the fuse used to fire their weapons, then he would give Moyano his food and lodging. Taking this on good faith, Moyano ordered his men to extinguish the fuses. As soon as this was done, the old chief let out a loud shout, and a few hundred warriors, now well armed, descended on the soldiers from the woods. Moyano and all but one of his men were slaughtered. This time, Juan Martín de Badajóz, alias Juancinto, was not the sole survivor and witness. A Spaniard named Calderon escaped and swam over 20 miles to deliver the news of the massacre to Santa Elena.

The day the swimmer arrived corresponded with the arrival from San Augustín of Hernando de Miranda, the superior of the newly appointed Govenor, Alonso Solis. On receiving news of the disaster from the swimmer Calderon, everyone, including all the farm families, retreated to within the walls of the fort. It was noted that one farmer's son had not returned after foraging for food. With the loss of Moyano and his 21 soldiers, that left only 27 soldiers to defend the fort. Despite these poor odds, Hernando de Miranda sent Governor Solis out with nine men to find the missing boy. The Indians attacked the search party, and again, killed all but one witness. The witness returned to the fort and reported the catastrophe. Soon thereafter, Fort San Felipe was attacked by over 500 Indians. The colonists responded with harquebuses and cannon fire; the Indians withdrew to the nearby woods. After two days of waiting for another, perhaps the final attack, Miranda ordered a total exodus from the fort and island. All the colonists and soldiers were rowed out to a large vessel anchored in deep water. From there, they watched Santa Elena burn.

Teresa Martin and her two daughters, Ines, and Teresa, fled on this boat to San Augustín. Teresa Martín de Badajoz remained a widow in San Augustín for three more decades until the end of her life. There, in 1600, she was officially interviewed along with two other survivors who had participated in the Pardo Expedition. The other two were Juan de Ribas, a soldier who had accompanied Captain Pardo on his second expedition and returned with him to Santa Elena. The other survivor was de Ribas's wife, Luisa Mendez, an Indian woman who was taken hostage by Moyano, perhaps at Chisca.

Teresa testified that after 32 years she remembered that Captain Pardo, during his second expedition before leaving Fort San Juan, told the garrison and the town that he would return . . . "within three or four moons," that is, within two and a half or three and a half months. Teresa told the interviewer that when Juan Pardo did not return by mid-March, "some of the men began to commit indiscretions with local women, angering their men."

Quhana lamented that she never again saw her father after going to Santa Elena to be with her husband. Her daughters now were grown and married, one to a Spanish soldier and the other to a Spanish merchant. She spent much time gazing out over the water from San Augustín remembering Juancinto and all the amazing stories he told. And then there was his music. She reflected on his last mission and smiled despite the pain in her heart. That last mission to secure food from the village of Escamacu claimed his life. The real mission that crowned his life was the delivery of the story of the destruction of the forts to the ears of Juan Pardo and Adelasntado Menéndez. Quhana took heart in the knowledge that since Juancinto's delivery of the devastating report, the Spanish had been afraid to venture again into the interior of her land.

CHAPTER 16

FONTE FLORA

APRIL-MAY 1568

The four departed in the moonlight, walking west toward Table Rock. On the dark horizon, the landmark appeared to Davide as a small black anvil against the moon-lit indigo sky. Xequina, in the lead, carried a torch in one hand and the other hand, a large basket with personal items, blankets, and cooking utensils. Over her shoulder and down her back was one of her father's hunting bows, and on her belt, a quiver with arrows.

With each step Xequina was confirmed in her resolve: *'I have no doubt that the Spirit leads me to be with these three. Ayo, bless his heart, made a special trip to warn us to escape and hide in a cave up in the Gorge. I must trust Ayo, and someday he will be a great War Chief and perhaps the Mico. But he is not for me. I have my man. Now we must establish ourselves where Ayo said and always be on good terms with Joara, although we can never live there again. I am sure Ruy and I will have many children, strong, healthy, and intelligent. Perhaps we will be a new tribe. I will soon dance with the Spirit and with the man I love.'*

Xequina was contemplating the above when she heard an explosion coming from Joara, behind her. They all turned and saw the eastern sky aglow.

"That is the powder from the storeroom in the fort," Ruy says. "It's all over."

"Are we the only survivors?" Davide wondered aloud. Nothing more was said.

They proceeded in the direction of the shadow of the black anvil on the western horizon. Vara was carrying two baskets balanced on each side of a stick riding on her shoulders. One basket contained ears of corn, hickory nuts, and chestnuts, along with an assortment of cooking and medicinal herbs. In the other basket, she carried extra clothes and gardening tools with personal treasures and mementos from her family.

She thought of her family as she traveled with the others. '*Father and Erbani saw this coming, and I suppose I did too. Davide and I never talked about the idea of an uprising, but it seemed to be no surprise even to him. After this, Davide and I will not have to worry about getting married at the Green Corn Ceremony, or any of the problems that Xequina had. Those problems are now solved for us, as we are outcasts, but that's not so bad. I love Davide, and he loves me. We are meant for each other. We also have Xequina and Ruy with us. Together we will be fine. We will all have to work to keep ourselves fed with game, fish, corn, beans, and squash. Davide is wise, and with Ruy they have many stories from the round world which they will impart to our children.*'

Both Ruy and Davide carried their leather army satchels with blankets and each one with a crossbow stolen from the fort. They had a limited number of lead projectiles but intended to design their own bullets and arrows when the lead was gone.

The moon disappeared behind Table Rock as the foursome came upon the Gorge River.

In the darkness by the riverbank, just before dawn, they decided to rest for a few hours to recoup their energy. They rose with the rising sun and refreshed themselves in the bold little river, then ate some cornbread before they proceeded west along the river trail. Xequina and Vara judged that they were about two miles upstream on the Gorge River from where it flowed into the Catawba, and maybe eight miles, as the crow flew, across rolling hills to Joara. They were not far the entrance into the gorge, with Table Rock looming ahead of them.

The hills became steeper and foreboding as they followed the river through the gap in the mountain range. At a beaver dam pool they crossed over to the west side of the river and soon found themselves on a high path above the tumbling waters. From that higher perspective they could now see the river, carving a canyon, the sides of which were a primeval forest with monstrous rock outcroppings. There was no sign of human life, no cookfires or river traffic.

Not more than three miles into the Gorge, they found the cave that Ayo had told Xequina about. The opening was not far from the riverbank and was on the side of a steep sloop. Once inside, the cave opened-up and the four went exploring. They decided to occupy only the first two rooms and to get rid of the varmints with a smoke fire which would also drive the bats from the ceiling.

At sundown, they cooked a large meal and ate it, then spread-out on their blankets to relax— Xequina in the arms of Ruy and Vara in the arms of Davide. All was well, and they gave thanks. The four were too tired for anything but sleep.

The next day, they set out to find the perfect place for their settlement. But there was a disagreement. Davide and Vara argued for finding a site farther up the Gorge for safety reasons, to be less in touch with the world at large and all its trouble, while Xequina cautioned that the farther up the Gorge they went, the farther into the unknown they would go. "And as Ayo said," she pointed out, "the Gorge is a land of outlaws, outcasts, witches, and wild beasts."

Ruy sided with Xequina. They believed that their cave three miles into the Gorge was safe enough, but they did not want to live like cave-people. They wanted contact with human beings, real people. They wanted contact with the Cherokee world up in the mountains and with the Catawba world down in the plains. They also needed flat land for cultivation with plenty of water. Vara and Davide were not convinced by this reasoning, so they struck-out along the high path following the river up farther into the Gorge, looking for a safer, more remote place to settle.

Xequina and Ruy retraced the path along the Gorge River from the previous day. With eyes open and their senses primed, they looked for the perfect place for the settlement that Xequina saw in her dreams. It was a splendid late-spring morning, cloudless with a slight breeze flowing along the river down from the headwaters on high, near the rock-face of the grandfather. The breeze carried the fire-fragrance of sap from the pine, hemlock, and cedar stands above, blended with the smell of earth from the rhododendron and laurel thickets along the banks of the Gorge River below.

Xequina and Ruy proceeded down the river. The Gorge began to open-up. On their right they found another bold creek which merged with the river. Ruy could see to the south beyond the creek that the land had flattened out with other small creeks defining a large meadow-land covered with spring flowers. The flowers on this morning were fresh and invigorating. Hand in hand, they splashed into the creek with joyous abandon and emerged wet in the morning sun. To the west beyond the meadow was a grassy knoll and beyond that, a small mountain.

Xequina whispered, "This must be what they call 'Yellow Mountain.'"

At the base of the grassy hill was a marshy area, and spreading out from the marsh were more acres of wildflowers, mostly yellow, about two feet high and buzzing with bees and activity. They walked through the meadow to the marsh, Ruy entered the soggy earth, exploring the bottom and kicking up mud. There in the marsh at the base of the hill he found a rock outcrop and the source of bubbling muck. On his hands and knees he removed the mud from the rock until clear water flowed. They stood back and watched.

"We are here!" said Xequina in Catawban.

Looking up, Ruy answered, "Xequina, we will build our home on that meadow above the spring."

They drank the clear water cupped in Ruy's hand, and then continued to walk in the meadow above the spring. They walked like wonder-struck lovers, like Adam and Eve in the Garden of Delights, crossing the large meadow of wildflowers and resting in the shade of a chestnut oak grove near the base of the mountain. Out of the corner of her eye Xequina caught sight of a family of deer crossing the flowered meadow below the spring and leaping over what appeared to be another creek on the western border of the field. This creek came falling out from the backside of Yellow Mountain. Ruy could see that their paradise was a triangle of flowered land, watered on two sides by bold creeks with a mountain as the backdrop. Below the meadow, the various streams joined the Gorge River. From further up the slope of Yellow Mountain, gazing to the south , the lovers could make out where the Gorge River joining the Catawba. Captured by the glory of the moment Ruy held Xequina's hand and with his other pointed toward the joining creeks and rivers. "Look, Xequina. We will build on this spot in paradise looking out over an inner triangle of meadows defined by creeks within an outer triangle of forests defined by two rivers."

Xequina exclaimed, "This is enough good land for a town the size of Joara!"

"For our new tribe!" Ruy rejoined.

Xequina looked at Ruy coquettishly and said, "Let's get busy making that tribe."

Hand in hand they started running down into the meadow, past the spring and the marsh surrounding it, and into the middle of the vast field of yellow flowers. They caught their breaths and collapsed in each other's arms laughing. Their leather clothes, still damp and with mud from the spring, were quickly removed. Their firm bodies disappeared in the sea of wildflowers, amidst the humming sounds of earth-life mixed with love sounds first whispered in Catawban and Portuguese, and then shouted to the heavens. The discipline of half a year of restrained passion was released like two oceans coming to meet at the tip of Africa. The Cape of Storms became the Cape of Good Hope.

In those magic moments, the first seed of a new tribe was germinated. Passions exhausted, the two lovers laid back among the flowers and gazed up into the cloudless morning sky with hands touching warm flesh. The fragrance of wildflowers, sweat and passion was profusive. The sounds of buzzing bees and a friendly hummingbird was interrupted by the caws of a group of crows circling overhead, curious at the sounds and sight of the lovely interruption in the field of flowers below.

As they slept in the warm, mid-morning sun, their pleasant nap among the flowers was interrupted by calls from Vara and Davide searching for them. Xequina and Ruy rose up, clothed themselves, and greeted their companions.

Previouisly Vara and Davide had walked along the treacherous path going up the river, and the land got more rugged and unacceptable the farther they trekked. They stopped to rest and Davide asked Vara if she remembered the day she flung the water moccasin back into the San Juan River.

She said, "yes".

"Do you remember what else you said?"

"No, what else.", Vara replied.

"You prayed or talked to Uktena, and asked him to protect me from snakebites, in exchange for letting the snake live."

"And you have not been bitten, right?"

"Yes, thank God. And you told me that Uktena was part snake, part bird, part fish and part man. And where did you tell me where Uktena lives?"

"Oh yes. I see where this is going.", she replied. "I told you Uktena likes to stay in the Gorge up beyond Table Rock."

"Right! So, I am telling you that I do *not* want to live where Uktena lives and all the unsavory creatures Ayo was talking about. Don't you agree?

Vara had to concede to this argument and so they turned and retraced their steps downriver intending to find Xequinqa and Ruy. They eventually found the same field of flowers that had captivated Xequina and Ruy. Realizing that this was the perfect place, they started shouting for their friends, hoping to announce their discovery.

They were not surprised to see the bare torsos of Ruy and Xequina rise from the field of flowers.

After putting on his clothes under cover of flowers, Ruy shouted to Davide, "I need to show you something!"

He led Davide up through the meadow, into the marsh, and to the source of the spring which he had uncovered. "Look! It flows with as much pure water as the *Fonte dos Amores* in the *Quinta das Lagrimas*.[14] I am going to clean-up this spring and tile it with flat rocks like the fountains in Coimbra. We are going to build up there on the hill between this spring here, and the mountain. You can join us if you want. There is plenty of land for all."

Vara and Davide stood in the flowers with their hands over their brows, shielding the morning sun and surveyed the area from Yellow Mountain and the range beyond dissected by the Gorge River.

Davide laughed and spoke. "Yes! This is the place, I can feel it in my bones! I can feel *Pai*[15] very close. I can still hear him shouting 'Lekh Lekha . . . Lekha, Lekh Lekha, Lekha . . . Lekha . . . Lekha . . . Lekha!'[16] as he slapped the shanks of our horses to begin our escape. Let's settle here and call it 'Lekh. Lekha.'"

Ruy thought for a moment and said, "No. No, Davide. That's not right. 'Lekh Lekha' meant to get out of here and start a new race of people, a new tribe, which is your destiny. But I object to naming our place "get out!" How can I forget that afternoon in the *Quinta das Lagrimas*, with the two fountains, one of Love, and one of Tears, and there was love and there were tears. But I now hear the Rabbi, your father, telling me to name our settlement, 'Fonte Flora,' after this very fountain among all these flowers."

They all agreed, and so Fonte Flora was founded, and through the generations settled.

CHAPTER 17

DANIEL AND IMMOKALEE

OLAMICO, FONTE FLORA AND RIVERS APRIL 1568- SUMMER 1605

After Juancinto left Canosaqui on his mission to Santa Elena, Daniel and Immokalee stayed with Quhana's parents until the Shaman told them it was safe for them to travel, and travel they must, for it was not their destiny to stay in Canosaqui. Suye'ti gave them a good canoe and sent them forth, down the river. They paddled the French Broad River, now familiar, for three days until they reached Immokalee's home on the island of Olamico, where her father, the Orata, and the townspeople received them well.

By now, Daniel had discarded most of the Spanish garments and vestiges of the Army. He did keep his knife, now important to keep his beard shaved to look more like a Creek or Cherokee Warrior. Another object worth salvaging was a set of cast iron measuring scales, found on the floor of the burned out kitchen at the fort in Cauchi.

Nine months on the island of Olamico and boredom and general restlessness began to work their way into the mood of the couple. However, instead of setting out for adventure, Daniel, now a married man with some expectation of maturity, had a plan. Inspired by thoughts of his parents, Ahmad and Bela, Daniel convinced Immokalee that they should try their hand at becoming river traders. This was a profession somewhat undeveloped on the big rivers flowing south down the big valleys on the western side of the great Appalachee Range.

Within a few years, Daniel and Immokalee became well-known for trading in commodities from as far north as the salt mines on the Holston River to the southern Coosa Chiefdom on the Coosa River. Much of their trade was on the on the Tanasqui or Tennessee River and its tributaries. On the Tennessee, Daniel refused to go beyond the town of Napochies or let any of his family do business south of this village. When asked the reason for this, he would not reply.

As year followed year, it became clear that the vocation of river traders fulfilled all the needs of Daniel and Immokalee, and together they were never lonely.

One secret of their growing success was the set of Spanish scales that they employed every day. They developed a reputation for giving a fair price for a fair measure. By this practice, they knew and managed to set fair prices for all commodities, but the ultimate secret of their success was the fact that they did not covet wealth. They loved what they were doing and were filled with the joy of living, being together, never lonely, raising children, being useful and of service to the people.

When Immokalee started having children, she stayed in Olamico, and Daniel traded alone. As his sons and daughters became of age, they would accompany him on his trading trips in canoes of their own, thus learning the trade.

It was at this time that Daniel, Immokalee, and family decided to load-up all the canoes and venture up the French Broad, paddling up-river and trekking where necessary along the river paths through the mountain gorges. They stopped to visit the elders in Canosaqui and then went on to see friends in Cauchi. Further on at Tocae they stored their canoes and walked down the eastern slope of the range, along the trails beside the headwaters of the Swannanoa and Catawba Rivers. Their destination was the junction of the Catawba and the Gorge River, there to spend time with their dearest friends and relatives at the growing village of Fonte Flora.

Their first reunion was so successful that Daniel and Immokalee and their family started making the two-week trip to Fonte Flora every year.

Immokalee and Daniel did not stop at four but eventually had seven children: four girls and three boys. In the early years of what they called the annual "*armada*," the older children would be responsible for the safety of the little ones. Beginning with that first "*armada,*" the yearly event took on the importance of a mating ritual.

Immokalee and Daniel made it known to their children that they would only condone a marriage to a mate from Fonte Flora, as if Olamico and Fonte Flora were the only two clans within a single tribe, which, in effect was the case. Fonte Flora, with a nucleus of two families, was growing much faster than the community at Olamico; therefore, the youth of Fonte Flora were encouraged to marry with the clan at Olamico, but were not prohibited from doing otherwise. One rule, common among the Cherokee and Catawba, was strictly enforced in Olamico and Fonte Flora: the groom went to live in the compound of the bride's family.

By the time Daniel had 60 years of age he was leading the annual flotilla to Fonte Flora with his four daughters, their husbands, and a dozen grandchildren. They would stay in Fonte Flora in the compounds of Daniel's three sons, who had married daughters of Ruy and Xequina and Davide and Vara. It was on one of those trips that Daniel and family stopped, as they always did, at the hot springs at Canosaqui. Suye'ti and his wife had long passed, but in his place Suye'ti had trained a young medicine man who now served the community. In a private session with the shaman, Daniel was diagnosed with an illness that he knew would soon take his life. At that time, he began to formulate a peculiar parting request.

Daniel wanted to celebrate his life, family, and friends while he was still active and capable. To this end, he requested that Fonte Flora and Olamico celebrate their annual reunion in the upcoming year in Olamico, and all agreed. When mid-summer arrived, the contingent from Fonte Flora paddled their canoes down the French Broad River through the mountains and down to the island of Olamico. After two days of festivities, Daniel announced that the celebration was not yet over. He told his assembled family and friends that he had heard the Great Spirit call and knew where he was to meet his destiny. It would entail a journey south along the French Broad River and then the Tanasqui River down to the village of the Napochies. From there, it was only a half-day paddle from where he was going. All were invited to journey down the rivers with him.

No one, except for Immokalee, had a clear intuition about the purpose of the journey and how it would end. Juancinto, now long passed, would have know if he had been there.

All set out in joyful comradery gathering the supplies for the long trip, but there was a strange, almost mournful excitement in the air. All wanted to be near Daniel and Immokalee, to hear their stories and sing their songs. Many would be going to places on the rivers that they had only vaguely heard about. That would be exciting, but the elders suspected that they would be coming back without Grandfather Daniel.

After a week of good weather, the flotilla reached the town of Napochies. They spent the night there, and the next morning set out cautiously in a single file to negotiate the twists as the big river found its way through the mountain trying to block it at every turn. Daniel and Immokalee were in the lead canoe. At about noon, they came in sight of Un'tiguhi, the boiling pot, and Suck Creek that fed it. Daniel guided his canoe to the right bank and the others followed. They made camp, had lunch, and some even had a nap.

The siestas were interrupted by the advent of the Thunder Boys. They came in dark clouds from the southwest. When they reached the river, they released their energy. The rain fell in sheets and soon engorged Suck Creek, which descended into the river like a waterfall. The signal could not be clearer. Daniel knew it was time. He got into his canoe, intending to shove off the bank. The grandchildren began to cry and pester their parents, who were all watching the patriarch intently. Ruy and Davide entered the water and pushed the canoe back to the bank, but contrary to their intention, when the canoe touched the bank Vara and Xequina helped Immokalee into Daniel's canoe.

She knelt in front of Daniel and pleaded, "You are my allotted man. Your soul is at the very center of my soul. If you go without me, my soul will be a hollow, lifeless shell."

Daniel replied, "They are calling for me. Are they calling for you too?"

"Yes, for we are one," she said.

"Are you not afraid?"

"No. With you I am not afraid, and I don't want to be without love, without you."

"Very well then, I am going to La Gran Copala. There we can dance on the roofs of the white buildings of the Golden City."

Immokalee, now smiling, and without taking her eyes off Daniel, untied the bowline from the canoe and let it slide into the water.

With his paddle, Daniel shoved off into the current, and in less than a minute the canoe had reached the outer ring of the vortex. Now without paddling, the whirlpool carried the canoe into the diminishing spiral, increasing in speed as it sunk into the river. Daniel and Immokalee kept their eyes transfixed on each other while the canoe, now spinning, began to take on water. Both Daniel and Immokalee raised their hands to bid farewell to those on the bank. Within seconds their heads were enveloped in the froth, leaving the last sight of two sets of hands waving farewell in all directions.

Daniel saw the diffused light from below and let his body sink toward it, his lungs now full of water. He looked around and realized that Immokalee was not by his side. He propelled upward until he saw her ankle, grabbed it, and pulled her down. He held her close in his arms until he felt life again begin to stir in her limbs. He kissed her lips, and her eyes opened, and then she smiled.

Hand in hand, they descended together toward the light, which got brighter and quite intense, like the noonday sun in the Moroccan desert. Daniel was expecting to see the white buildings of La Gran Copala, but what he saw were rolling white sand dunes. A seagull flew into their path, and they followed the bird until they saw below in the distance the blue waters of the Mediterranean.

The couple flew closer to the water, where they could make out the white sails of a merchant's vessel on the horizon. The lines of the ship were familiar to Daniel, and as they approached from above he realized that it was the *"Rainha de Alcântara,"* and he recognized some crew members he had not seen for 40 years. They were waving for the couple to join them and there, at the wheel, was his father Ahmad, with Bela, his mother. Daniel and Immokalee landed on the main deck, and Daniel ran like a young man to embrace his parents. He introduced the beautiful Immokalee to his parents and began telling them of the many stories from the New World.

***

The Shaman of Olamico once reported on a dream from the imaginal realm between Heaven and Earth. He saw a large boat with many sails that patrolled the rivers to the east and the west of the great

Blue Ridge divide. The vessel was in service to help river traders in trouble. The Shaman was informed by the great-grandchildren of Daniel and Immokalee that the boat was the "*Rainha de Alcântara*," manned by their ancestors.

EPILOGUE

From Belmonte

Rabbi Elias, Davide's father, stayed in Coimbra and married Dona Ida, the governess of Ana Sofia and servant in the Pedro Nunes household. Ana Sofia had the child, a boy, who went by the name of Ruy Nunes. Meanwhile, Toninho Cabral, also in Coimbra, became very close to the Nunes family and knowing well the full story, and with the belief that Ruy and Davide would never return, offered to marry Ana Sofia. She, eventually, conceded to the inevitable and accepted Toninho's offer, knowing that Toninho had the makings of a good man from whom she would never have to hide anything.

Ruy Nunes's name was changed to Ruy Nunes Cabral. Ana Sofia, Toninho, and the two grandfathers raised Ruy Nunes Cabral in Coimbra. The grandfathers, one a famous cosmologist, the other a rabbi-shepherd, became close friend and passed away peacefully and content in Ruy Nubes's 12th year. At which time Toninho and Ana Sofia moved with their son and twin daughters to Belmonte to take care of the Castle and the Cabral Estate. On his 15th birthday young Ruy Nunes Cabral, officially the great-grandson of the Navigator Cabral, vowed to one day find his birth father.

From Joara

Ruy and Xequina built their house at the foot of Yellow Mountain, overlooking the flower spring. Before their eyes, their ever-growing family extended into three generations. The area at the base of the mountain became known as Upper Fonte Flora.

Davide, Vara, and their extended family lived in Lower Fonte Flora in the flat, fertile flood-plain of the Gorge River, where it joined the Catawba River.

Daniel and Immokalee ventured every year from Olamico, with their armada of canoes paddling up-river and into the mountains to visit Fonte Flora. The summer trips eventually became a mating ritual not unlike the Green Corn Ceremony. A result of this was that many young men from Olamico, raised on the rivers beyond the mountains, would spend their married lives, farming, foraging, and hunting within a Catawba-Portuguese-Jewish culture, while many young men from Fonte Flora learned to live with their in-laws in Olamico, trading on the rivers in a Creek-Portuguese-Jewish environment.

The Chiefdom of Joara, after the elimination of Fort San Juan, rose further in prestige and power within the Catawba Nation. With the debris from the Spanish installations, the Sacred Ceremonial Mound at the square ground in Joara was doubled in diameter and height. But the ascendency of Joara was short-lived. By the end of the 16th century, the Catawba Nation had been devastated by an onslaught of smallpox, originally introduced by the de Soto Expedition. Culturally, Joara suffered by virtue of being located on principle east-west and north-south trading trails. Catawban ways were corrupted by traders who brought alcohol and firearms down from Richmond and up from Charleston. Within a century of the burning of Fort San Juan, Joara was abandoned, and soon after, with the birth of the United States of America, the Catawba Nation would be reduced to a small reservation on the Catawba River near the boundary between North and South Carolina.

****

In 1585, 17 years after the destruction of the Spanish forts, the English Crown, together with Sir Walter Raleigh, financed an attempt to establish a colony of 120 men, women, and children on Roanoke Island in the Albemarle Sound of North Carolina. After less than a year, the colony was on the verge of starvation when Sir Francis Drake, the famous English pirate, and a friend of Sir Walter Raleigh, sailed into Albemarle Sound. Drake's fleet, called the "Great Expedition," was originally composed of 25 ships and 2,300 men.

He was returning from a very successful campaign of raiding and looting Spanish and Portuguese colonies in Central and South America. Drake's maritime rampage included the following localities: the

Portuguese Brazilian coastal cities; the Spanish coastal cities of Columbia and Venezuela; the Caribbean islands and the Spanish settlements on the coast of La Florida, including San Augustín and Santa Elena. A Spanish prisoner from Drake's expedition recounted that Drake took "300 Indians from Cartagena, mostly women and 200 Negros, Turks, and Moors, who do menial service."

After looting both San Augustín and what was left of Santa Elena, Drake's next task on the Atlantic coast was to stop and visit the new English colony at Roanoke Island. One purpose for stopping at Roanoke Island was to deposit the extra Negro and Indian slaves he was carrying to serve as a labor force. Drake thought he would find a flourishing settlement at Roanoke Island, but instead he found 120 English colonists that were hungry and alienated from the surrounding Indian population. Fed-up with the New World, they demanded to return to England.

To make room for these returning ex-colonists, Drake left most of his cargo of human captives ashore. He returned to England with only 100 Turks, which Queen Elizabeth I either ransomed or repatriated to Turkey to win favor with the Ottoman Sultan, the enemy of her enemy Spain. Beyond these, it was recorded that only three West Africans arrived in England with Drake's fleet. If these figures are accurate, then potentially 400 South American Indians from Spanish and Portuguese colonies and 100 West African Negroes and Moors were left to fend for themselves on Roanoke Island.

***

A year after Drake's fleet departed from Roanoke Island, in a second attempt at a colony, 115 men, women, and children arrived on the island in 1586. There was no sign of the captives Drake had left on the island the year before. A re-supply visit in 1587 found the latest colony of 115 people vacated with only the word "Croatan" carved on a post, inspiring the legends of the "Lost Colony."

There is good evidence that this Lost Colony of 115 people were assimilated into various tribes such as the Lumbee Tribe of Eastern North Carolina where the existence of old English surnames is prevalent among this population. But the greater question is: <u>What happened to the 500 South American Indians, West African Negroes, and Moors that had</u>

<u>been castaway in 1585?</u> If it is true, as documents written at the time indicate, that in 1585 Sir Francis Drake discharged most of his human cargo at Roanoke Island, then where did hundreds of souls from South America and the Caribbean, speaking Spanish, Portuguese, Turkish and African dialects, go?

Obviously, the groups would have gone west to the mainland, and from there, if they continued west, they would have progressed along the boundary that would later separate the states of Virginia from North Carolina. As historical accounts suggest, they integrated with tribal elements from the Powhatan, the Saponi, the Oconeechee, the Tutelo, the Saura, the Wins, and the "Portugee," and more broadly with the Catawba, the Cherokee, and the Yuchi.

The fates of these castaway remnants, whether assimilated into tribes or retaining separate cultural identities, would have been the same as that of the original Indian communities, meaning they would have been pushed ever-westward by the predominant northern European colonial population. They would have been pushed, valley after valley, from the fertile river floodplains to the thin-soiled barren mountain ridges. One of the names which evolved to identify these various groups was "Melungeon."

This term is possibly derived from the Portuguese word, "melungo," meaning shipmate, or the Turkish word. "melun-căn," meaning cursed soul or one whose luck has run out. A combination of both translations goes a long way in describing the plight of these isolated communities over the past 500 years; these ancient communities of disputed origin which were not quite Indian, not quite black, and not quite white.

***

The following is a paraphrased description that was published in 1912.

The Melungeons are a peculiar people living in the mountains of Eastern Tennessee, Western North Carolina, Southwestern Virginia, and Western Kentucky, and are of queer appearance and uncertain origin.

They have a swarthy complexion, straight black hair, black or grey eyes, native Indian eyes are always black, and are not tall but heavy set. They call themselves Portuguese (which they pronounce "Porter-ghee") and are found in regions mentioned by our first pioneers of civilization there.

***

In our story, which is at root historical fiction, the name "Fonte Flora," over time, would morph into "Fonta Flora," which was and is an actual place with historical reality. Fonta Flora in Western North Carolina, once flourished at the mouth of the Linville Gorge, where that river used to flow into the Catawba River. Now, that is, since 1919, a large part of this once thriving multi-racial settlement lies under the waters of Lake James, created to provide energy for an advancing civilization. During the passage of time, the strangely unique settlement of Fonta Flora had taken-on immigrants from the populations of freed and runaway black slaves, as well as neighboring Indians, whites, and wanderers from many colors and origins.

The one-time thriving community of Fonta Flora, west of Morganton, North Carolina, could easily fall into the catch-all category of Melungeon, however, in the light of its location, only 20 miles west from where Joara and Fort San Juan once existed, the origin of Fonta Flora is quite possibly strangely unique unto itself.

3' high remains of Joara's original 20' high ceremonial mound.

Site of the village of Joara taken from the ceremonial mound.

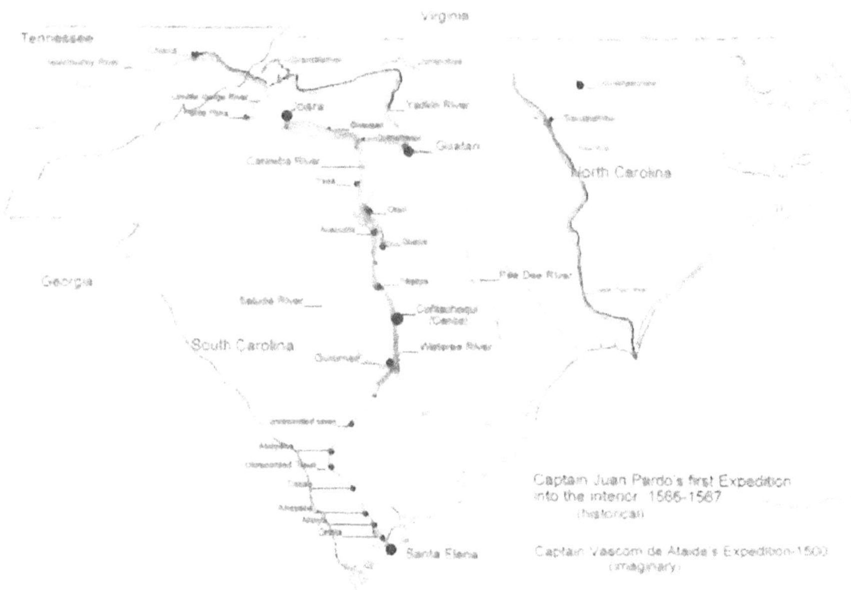

Image C Caption: Captain Juan Pardo's first expedition into the interior, 1566-1567.

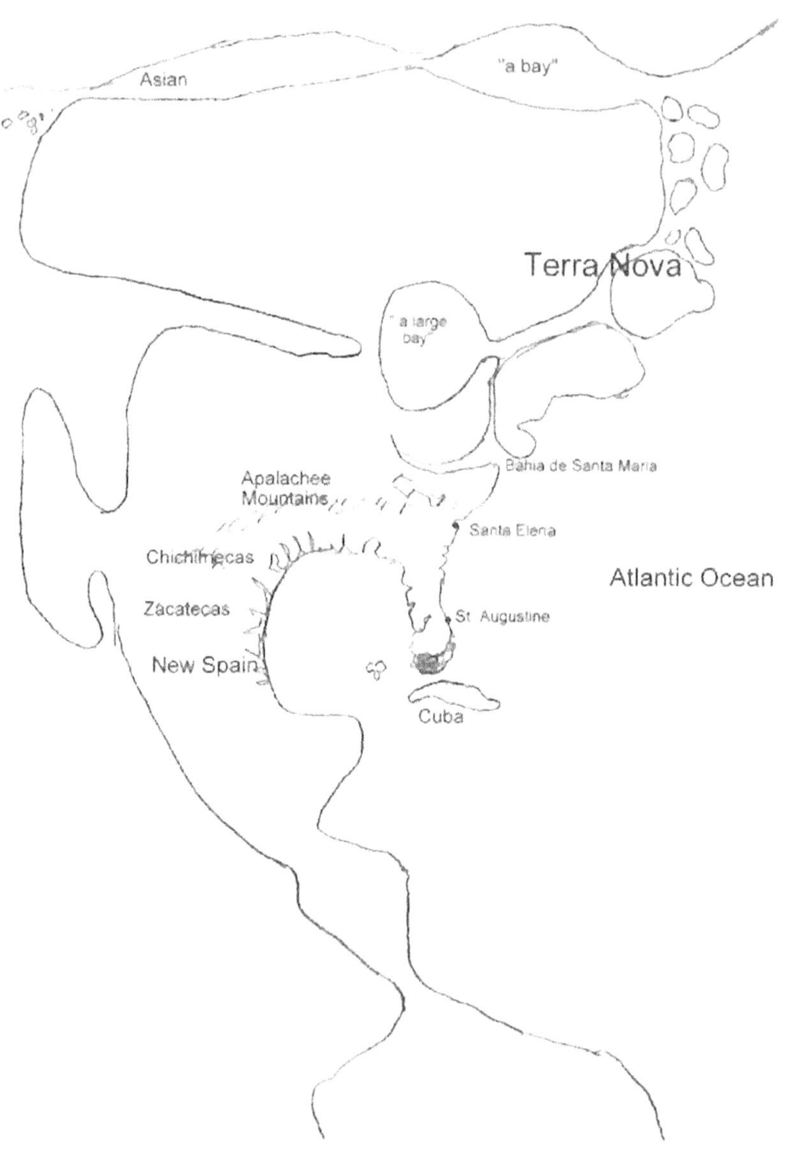

16th-century Spanish misconception about the geography of North America. Adapted from map found in *The Spanish Jesuit Mission in Virginia, 1570-1572.*, by Clifford M. Lewis and Albert H. Loomie.

Recommended Reading and Acknowledgement

By Charles Hudson, anthropologist and historian who passed away in 2013.

The Juan Pardo Expeditions, 1990, 2005.

Knights of Spain, Warriors of the Sun, 1997.

Conversations with the High Priest of Coosa, 2003 (a novel)

The Southeastern Indians, 1976.

By the three anthropologists dedicated to uncovering the reality of Joara, Davide G. Moore, Robin A. Beck and Christopher B. Rodning.

Fort San Juan and the Limits of Empire, 2016

By James Mooney (1861-1921). Self-styled "ethnographer"/anthropologist/historian, Mooney spent years with the Eastern Band, learning various dialects of the Cherokee, hearing first-hand and recording histories, stories, myths, remedies, prayers and formulas from famous story-tellers and shamans, such as the legendary "Swimmer" and John Az and Taquadihi.

History, Myths and Sacred Formulas of the Cherokee, 1886-1887 (700 pages)

For personal knowledge, inspiration and encouragement in the writing of *Joara* , I want to express gratitude to my life-long friend, Nancy McIntyre, who recently passes away. Her father's line was Cherokee. Nancy shared life, wrote and danced deep in the North Carolina mountains in what once was, and still is, Cherokee country.

NOTES

1 A particular Portuguese form of homesickness.

2 Ceremony of Scratching. <u>Historical Myths and Sacred Formulas of the Cherokees</u>, p. 476, James Mooney

3 Paraphrased from Kana'ti and Selu myth found in <u>History, Myths, and Sacred Formukas of the Cherokee,</u> by James Mooney. There are many versions of this classic myth.

4 'Nokfilaki' was a Cherokee term used in the days of de Soto. It meant ' sea-foam person from the east.'

5 As the term "flamenco" was not used until the late 19th century, I am using the term "palos gitanos" to refer to the gypsy style of dance and guitar playing in the Andalusia area of Spain.

6 Adapted from prayer 'Concerning Living Humanity (Love), from History, Myths, and Sacred Formulas of the Cherokees. James Mooney, 1885

7 History, Myths, and Sacred Formulas of the Cherokees, p. 494. James Mooney. 1885

8 A version found in History, Myths and Sacred Formulas of the Cherokee, by James Mooney

9 Romany is the gypsy language.

10 "cante" is used as a song defining ones' life story or soul.

11 Formula for Separation (of Lovers), Sacred Formulas of he Cherokee, James Mooney

12 Raven Mocker. In Cherokee belief, one who robs the dying man of his life. The man who becomes a Raven Mocker takes a dying man's heart out and eats it, adding to his own life the quantity of days or years thay have taken from their victim. Myrhs of the Cherokee, p.402. James Mooney

13 Fort "Our Lady" and the town of "New Hope".

14 The Fountain of Lovers in the Garden of Tears

15 father

16 "Lekh Lekha!" . See Genesis 12:1-17:27 YHVH said to Abram, "Go you forth from your birthland to the land that I will show you."